The Living Edge
A wanderer's guide to Wenlock Edge

National Trust

Lower Dinchope

Foreword

by Marcus Halliwell, National Trust General Manager, South Shropshire

South Shropshire marks the boundary between lowland England and upland Wales. It is the backdrop for historical sagas and countless legends, its place names conjure up images of England of the imagination, now largely disappeared. It is an area with one of the lowest population densities in the country where star gazing is largely unaffected by light pollution. An area famous for its diverse countryside and wildlife, it brings to mind a lowland landscape made up of a patchwork of wheat fields, grazing and woodland with monumental oaks and six feet wide hazel and holly hedges. The ground then rises to the heather-topped Shropshire Hills, designated as an Area of Outstanding Natural Beauty with wind-sculpted hawthorns and wizened alders. As a place of contrasts, the area boasts the birthplace of the Industrial Revolution at Coalbrookdale and is known as the geological capital of England; the rocks and minerals deposits have affected human activity for millennia.

In keeping with the area, National Trust properties in South Shropshire are equally diverse, each representing what is special about its place in the landscape and history. In the east with the influence of the River Severn is Dudmaston, a complete traditional Shropshire estate centred around the house, garden and park, noted for its unusual modern art collection with its woodlands managed for timber production and nature conservation. Although smaller, Morville is in an idyllic location and Benthall has an industrial connection with nearby Ironbridge. To the west are large holdings of countryside in the Shropshire Hills Area of Outstanding Natural Beauty; the iconic Wenlock Edge with Wilderhope Manor, now a popular Youth Hostel famed for its view up the Apedale. The Long Mynd, an area of upland heath, has been a huge conservation success, Hopesay Hill and Walcot Wood are little-known but important sites.

The common link between all these places is the Outdoors, whether that is garden, park, woods, countryside, heath, hill or valley. We have thousands of acres and although almost half a million people visit our properties in South Shropshire every year, this fantastic resource is under-utilized. We are an organisation known for our country houses and gardens but I am not sure that we are known as a leading nature conservation and access charity, the second largest land owner in the country. We know that many people do not think that what we do is relevant to them.

We are working hard to change this perception. We want people to see these wonderful places as *their* places where they can have fun, adventure or just relax and unwind. There is space for everyone. We are working outside the boundaries of our properties with communities, asking them to get involved and in turn getting involved ourselves. In 2012 the Trust launches a campaign which celebrates the Outdoors. National Trust in South Shropshire will be leading the way by encouraging walking, running, cycling and camping. We think that now more than ever, these wonderful places can provide an antidote to the strains and pressures of modern life. We would like to reacquaint people with the Great Outdoors.

Published in 2011 in the United Kingdom by:

National Trust, Carding Mill Valley, Church Stretton, Shropshire SY6 6JG

Volume & Text © National Trust 2011
Images © individual photographers (see Acknowledgements, page. 211)

ISBN 978 0 7078 0421 7

Design by MA Creative, Shrewsbury. Printed in the UK by Cambrian Printers Ltd.

National Trust is a registered charity No. 205846

Wenlock Edge: west along Eaton Coppice

The Living Edge
A wanderer's guide to Wenlock Edge

Contents

The Living Edge – A wanderer's guide to Wenlock Edge · National Trust

Introduction

Twenty miles long and recognisable from space, Wenlock Edge is well-known in the West Midlands. It may be the longest continual strip of woodland in the UK, its geology is world famous and the boundary of the Shropshire Hills Area of Outstanding Natural Beauty has been stretched to include the Edge and its northern neighbour the Wrekin. National Trust first became involved with Wenlock Edge in 1936, when John Cadbury restored Wilderhope Manor and placed it in the care of the Trust to be used as a youth hostel, which it still is today.

In the 1980s National Trust started to acquire sections of Wenlock Edge in order to safeguard it from the threat of quarrying. Over 12 separate acquisitions between then and now have pieced together a continuous piece of woodland in a single ownership between Roman Bank in the south and Edge Wood to the north of Much Wenlock. As a unit of land it is possibly unique; at 8 miles long, an average of a quarter mile wide and most of it at an angle of about 40 degrees. More significantly this has been an example of where National Trust has been able to achieve gains at a landscape scale for nature conservation, landscape and access.

Over the last 20 years National Trust have maintained the integrity of the landscape and improved public access along a considerable length of the Edge. The woodland management has allowed plant and animal species dependant on this habitat to move freely within it and to spread from it along hedgerows and linking woodlands. Wenlock Edge is a large reservoir of woodland life and a giant wildlife corridor across South Shropshire.

Most of this land is ancient semi-natural woodland, largely ash with some hazel coppice. Previous landowners have planted conifers as a cash crop in some compartments. National Trust are harvesting these, allowing the native ash woodland to return. In fact, in some places ash trees march in to reclaim their rightful place. Of the total woodland area, 5% has been left unmanaged to become the wildwood of the future, perhaps in several hundred years from now. 90% is managed for 'high standards' productive timber (tall straight trees) and diverse habitat and 5% is managed as coppice, reflecting its former management, to produce sticks and hedging stakes.

The stewardship of the woodland has been planned by my colleague Alistair Heath with advice from Ray Hawes (National Trust head of woodlands) and supported by Chris Dunkerley. Ray has written on how the woods have developed in the past and how they might change in the future.

In places along the Edge there are delightful meadows and pockets of flower-rich grassland. Often these are on the old quarry workings; where grazing animals are present these grassland remain open although many have been lost to woodland already. These are visible in the woods as spoil heaps and exposed rock faces. It is ironic now, that for the last 10 years National Trust and the current quarry owners Bardon Aggregates have been working together to create flower-rich grassland. Hardy Hebridean sheep graze on newly developing grassland and nibble back scrub and young trees. At the time of writing National Trust and Bardon are discussing the future of these quarries, with the hope that they will be open to the public and linked to main body of the Edge in National Trust ownership.

Wenlock Edge has many stories and secrets, this book has a good collection of them told by people who know it well. There will, no doubt, be many more stories and we would love to hear them.

I hope you enjoy this book, it has been a labour of love for the authors and Trust staff. I hope that reading it encourages you to wander along the "Living Edge" in all seasons and in all weathers and to discover for yourself the mood and spirit of the place.

Peter Carty
NT Countryside, Park and Garden Manager – South Shropshire

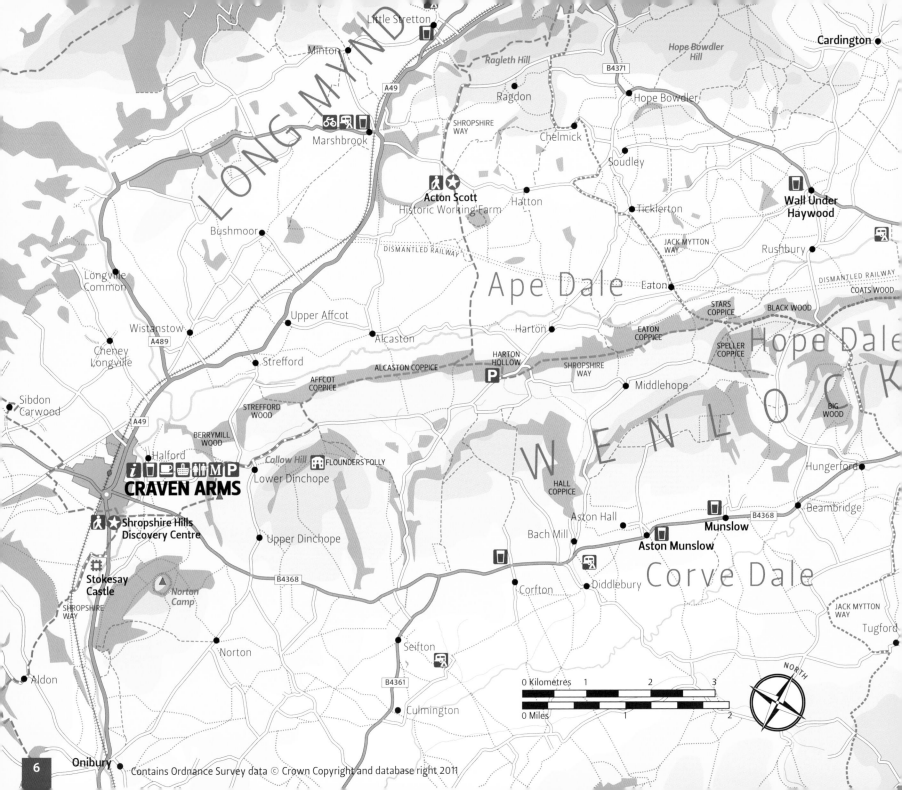

LONG MYND

Little Stretton

Minton

Cardington

Ragleth Hill

Hope Bowdler Hill

Ragdon

B4371

Hope Bowdler

Marshbrook

A49

SHROPSHIRE WAY

Chelmick

Soudley

Ticklerton

Wall Under Haywood

Acton Scott
Historic Working Farm

Hatton

JACK MYTTON WAY

Bushmoor

Rushbury

DISMANTLED RAILWAY

Ape Dale

Eaton

DISMANTLED RAILWAY

COATS WOOD

Longville Common

Harton

STARS COPPICE

BLACK WOOD

Upper Affcot

Alcaston

EATON COPPICE

Hope Dale

Wistanstow

A489

SPELLER COPPICE

Cheney Longville

HARTON HOLLOW

Strefford

ALCASTON COPPICE

SHROPSHIRE WAY

Middlehope

WENLOCK

AFFCOT COPPICE

BIG WOOD

Sibdon Carwood

A49

STREFFORD WOOD

BERRYMILL WOOD

Callow Hill

FLOUNDERS FOLLY

HALL COPPICE

Hungerford

Halford

Lower Dinchope

i I M P

CRAVEN ARMS

Aston Hall

Munslow

B4368

Beambridge

Shropshire Hills
Discovery Centre

Upper Dinchope

Bach Mill

Aston Munslow

Stokesay Castle

SHROPSHIRE WAY

Norton Camp

B4368

Corfton

Diddlebury

Corve Dale

JACK MYTTON WAY

Tugford

Norton

Seifton

Aldon

Culmington

B4361

NORTH

0 Kilometres   1   2   3

0 Miles   1   2

Onibury

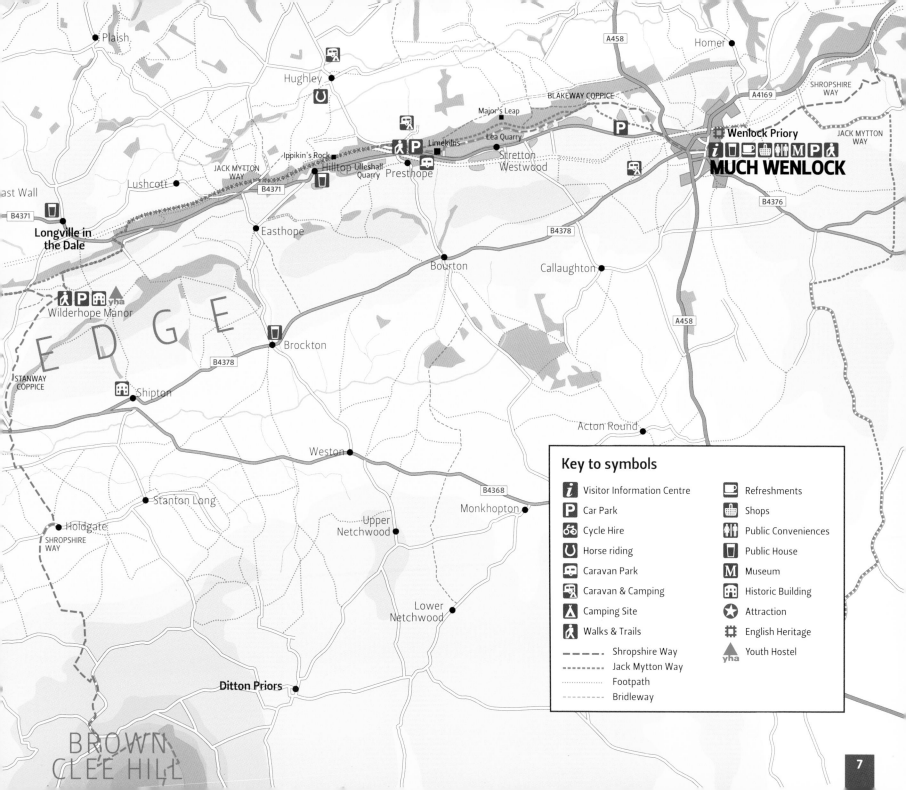

Plaish

Homer

A458

A4169

SHROPSHIRE WAY

Hughley

BLAKEWAY COPPICE

JACK MYTTON WAY

Major's Leap

Lea Quarry

Wenlock Priory

Stretton
Westwood

MUCH WENLOCK

Ippikin's Rock

JACK MYTTON
WAY

Hilltop   Lilleshall
         Quarry   Presthope

Limekilns

B4376

East Wall

Lushcott

B4371

B4378

B4378

B4371

Easthope

Bourton

Callaughton

Longville in
the Dale

A458

Wilderhope Manor

E   D   G   E

Brockton

STANWAY
COPPICE

B4378

Shipton

Acton Round

Weston

Holdgate

SHROPSHIRE
WAY

Stanton Long

B4368

Monkhopton

Upper
Netchwood

Lower
Netchwood

Ditton Priors

BROWN
CLEE HILL

Key to symbols

i	Visitor Information Centre		Refreshments
P	Car Park		Shops
	Cycle Hire		Public Conveniences
	Horse riding		Public House
	Caravan Park	**M**	Museum
	Caravan & Camping		Historic Building
	Camping Site		Attraction
	Walks & Trails		English Heritage
– – –	Shropshire Way	**yha**	Youth Hostel
·······	Jack Mytton Way		
··········	Footpath		
- - - -	Bridleway		

The Living Edge

by Paul Evans

Wenlock Edge stretches in a 20 mile-long ridge, from the birthplace of the Industrial Revolution in the Severn Gorge to the gateway to the Welsh Marches in Craven Arms. It is a very Shropshire phenomenon, an axis linking diverse and distinctive landscapes through this one diverse, distinctive land. With the Wrekin to the north, the Clee Hills to the east, the Stretton Hills to the west and Clun Forest to the south, Wenlock Edge acts as the spinal column through which impulses, from nerves ending in stones, ditches, bogs, trees, fields, hedges and the wild lives of this land, pass. It acts as a synaptic corridor, through which flash the sparks of being which give this land its spirit.

This is a kind of ecological view of what makes the spirit of a place. The received wisdom from ecology is about inter-connectedness, or as the pioneer ecologist John Muir once wrote, "Everything is hitched to everything else." Maybe things could exist on their own in isolation; possibly this tree, that hill, or these streams? In reality however, things don't; their existence is contingent on the relationships between them. In common with other landscape features, Wenlock Edge is made of such relationships, but there are certain characteristics created by natural processes, human activity and a wild spirit which arcs between them, giving the Edge its edge. This occurs within dimensions of space as well as time, a lot of time.

What we think of now as Wenlock Edge was once reef and shallow sea; 425 million years ago it was a living ecosystem inhabited by creatures which built a world for themselves out of lime, absorbing the water's calcium to protect themselves. Their limestone has lasted through all time since. From its origins on a latitude with present-day Australia, through world-shifting processes of plate tectonics, this great slab of stone tipped up here. The Edge is a wave of bone on which the centuries lean. It lives differently now.

Seen from the west, it is a dark brow of trees because along the breaking face of the wave are the woods of Wenlock Edge; the longest unbroken length of woodland

Brown Clee and Wenlock Edge from Hill End

in England. Under its roots the Edge rises 200-300 feet above the land, northeast to southwest, behind it the weight pushes westward, as if it were a tsunami about to break across the lowlands and smash into the hills of Wales. But the wave remains petrified, poised along its ridge, weathering, glacier-carved, bitten into by human endeavour, yet persisting. The wave is stilled, it is time that is tidal.

The sea creatures which created this stone belong to a time that geologists call the Silurian era; they remain as fossils. The submarine lime world they created is now released by water, ingested by the billions of organisms which make the lives of plants and animals possible; they also create a potent underworld from their deaths in the soil. Lime is liberated by people for their industry and agriculture through crushing and burning the stone. It was painted on sacred buildings; the Welsh *'Gwen'* which became the *'Wen'* in Wenlock means white, *'loc'* or *'lock'* means monastery. It is the lunar-white stuff of spiritual imagination made from Silurian sea-life.

Lime is also the sediment of settlement. People have settled on Wenlock Edge for thousands of years using what they found here to surround and protect themselves, just as those delicate sponges, coral polyps, sea-lilies and molluscs did in that ancient sea. Limestone has been quarried here for two thousand years at least. In Much Wenlock, the Priory church built in the mid 13th century stands on the Cluniac priory built in 1080, which stands on Leofric's Church built in 1050, which stands on Milburga's Abbey of 680, which may stand on a 2nd century Romano-British religious house, itself on a Celtic shrine. In Much Wenlock Museum, the carved limestone face of a local deity looks out from the other side of two millennia. Her gaze is steady, persistent and inscrutable; she gives nothing away. A lump of stone the

Wenlock Edge from Harley Bank

size of a fist, her face is a fossil of a whole culture in this landscape.

Across all those years, the dust, duff and middens pile on top of each other in strata, each layer holding its own stories, ideas and beliefs. Nothing is lost, all is buried in the sediment of soil and civilisation. The weight of history presses down to harden the rind which covers Wenlock Edge. We scrabble about on it, finding clues to secrets we don't know what to do with. We dig holes into the past.

In his poem, *'In Praise of Limestone'*, WH Auden, wrote, "...when I try to imagine a faultless love / Or the life to come... what I see is a limestone landscape." Auden may have been writing about the limestone landscape of the North Pennines, but there is something about

thyme flower in the sun, hart's tongue and polypody ferns green the shadows, jackdaws and peregrine falcons nest on high ledges. Cliff faces and scree slopes, pools and flushes, heaps, pits and terraces; all these places are being colonised by a wild life that bleeds onto clean open pages of stone from the margins. The pastures and meadows rich in wildflowers and invertebrates which are special to limestone soils have been decimated by modern agriculture and development. Only scraps and verges remain as refuges for wildlife; they are finding their ways into redundant quarries like exiles returning to a land scarred by the battlefields of a very long war. The products of the quarries: stone walls, mortar, lime-wash, road mettle and concrete create places for lichens, spleenworts, pellitory-of-the-wall and mason bees. Plants and animals have always reclaimed cracks in the landscape; however brutally it was purged or however tidily maintained, Nature is resurgent and opposed to our control.

the character of the stone which shapes the character of the people who dwell on it here too. For Auden, "The best and worst never stayed here long," those with a heroic, militaristic or nomadic bent went off to granite wastes, clay and gravel plains or the sea. Those who remained, the "inconstant ones", inhabited a land of external beauty which was not what it appeared to be, "this land is not the sweet home that it looks, / Nor its peace the historical calm of a site / Where something was settled once and for all."

Perhaps something has been settled. The last limestone quarry has closed. A long history of building the sacred and the profane from the stuff Wenlock Edge is made of has come to an end. There was nothing to mark its passing. The dust is settling and the wild is taking root in it again. In abandoned quarries, bee orchids and wild

Shropshire's great celebrant of Nature, the novelist poet and mystic Mary Webb, spent her formative years on Wenlock Edge. She would walk a mile from The Grange into Much Wenlock, "down a country road, beside which ran a thread of a brook, except in the summer. In the hedge banks grew a few sweet violets, and there you might find the largest, most brightly-coloured snail shells I have ever seen." Few would risk their children walking the same road today. The world may be a different place now and although there are still violets and snail shells where Mary Webb saw them, the simple charm of their appearance in her writing has a different meaning now. Greater than their role as natural treasures, they have gathered a symbolic power which lies in part to being opposed to the modern world. If wildlife is a charm to ward off the Nature-denying tendencies of consumerism, it has failed. So much of the ecological weave of the countryside has unravelled that the once commonplace is now extraordinary, making wildlife refuges such as Wenlock Edge even more significant.

Until 1895, when she was fourteen and still called Gladys Meredith, these lanes, fields, woods and streams on Wenlock Edge were Mary Webb's world. Her observations of Nature and instincts for a wild pantheism running through the land began to take shape here. So did her feelings for country people and the dramas of their lives. Even standing on the threshold of the twentieth century, she looked to places like Much Wenlock, which she described as "a very Rip-van-Winkle of a borough"; to smoke rising from hearths which were still remote, self-contained,

steeped in folklore, superstition and religious bigotry; on the cusp of the change to mechanised agriculture, travel and mass communication. She was absorbing a vibrant, ecologically rich countryside with a visceral and mystical wildness, soon to vanish or radically change. When she moved from The Grange, she packed these things up, folding the landscapes of her childhood into memory, her 'land within', taking all the things she needed to become Mary Webb the novelist and poet, adding to them everywhere she tried to put down roots. Mary Webb Country, her literary fiefdom, is thought of as southwest Shropshire but it is from the Edge that she would first see that land and feel connected to it. Nowhere would be as rich, vibrant and lost to her as the landscapes of her childhood. Her writing strained to return there; it became a song, a ballad for wild things

and stubborn spirits which refused to be exorcised from the modern world. Beyond the written word, the inspiration for that song can be heard, if we listen for it, carried on the wind through trees.

"On Wenlock Edge, the wood's in trouble," wrote AE Housman in *'A Shropshire Lad'*. Unlike Mary Webb, Housman was not one of ours. Scholarly but less ecologically literate, he thought he'd discovered a land of lost content and set about colonising landscapes he couldn't comprehend; his famous poem has held Shropshire in a cultural headlock since 1896. Housman imagined a Roman from *'Uricon'*; (Viraconium, now Wroxeter), watching a storm bending trees on Wenlock Edge. The storm linked Housman and the Roman to that place through "the old wind in the old anger", bending history as well as trees; "the tree of man was never quiet", stirring up ghosts. These trees have always been storm-catchers and when winds come barrelling in over hills and plains, trouble lives in the woods of Wenlock Edge.

The winds have blown through trees here since the early Holocene period 10,000 years ago. After the Ice Age, the forests of lime, ash, elm, cherry and hazel colonised from the still-connected continent. With them came creatures, many we are still familiar with, others which exist only in the fearful shadows of our imaginations. With people came fire and the axe; over thousands of years the amount of tree cover along the Edge has varied with the tides of time. Sometimes trees were felled and woods were sparse: trees cut for timber or charcoal or fodder; trees cut for pasture, quarrying or lime-burning; trees cut for bridleways or roads; trees cut by disease, like elms in the 1970s. At other times the woods returned as a shaggy pelt to the escarpment. Today there may be more trees and denser woods than there

Dove Plantation, Easthope

have been for centuries. Except for a few roads cutting up the steep bank, they form an unbroken twenty-mile line. This wooded axis is the living edge between past and present, presence and absence, light and darkness, myth and reality.

"A culture is no better than its woods," wrote Auden. What do the woods of Wenlock Edge say about our culture? They say we need a place where Nature can be free of our obsessions of control and exploitation and where we can find freedom within it: a place for wildlife and people together; a place of moods and shadows which changes with the seasons and not with our intentions; a place from which our culture sprang and still holds truths, desires and fears. Perhaps these woods also say our idea of the sacred has returned there; to the wild, through trees into the earth, the waters and the stone which inspired it.

Stars Coppice, hoar frost

Landscape
& Seasons:
Winter

A grey-blue peregrine falcon arrows through a grey-blue sky and lands on a ledge of grey-blue rock in Shadwell Quarry. Colours bleed into an inky wash but there is energy in the air, it is movement which gives this landscape definition. The peregrine bolts through the sky as a fall of stones rumbles down the rock-face into the blue pool below. Ripples on the water, sound-waves through the air; they tremor through the body and are snatched up by the wind.

Lower Dinchope

These are wet and windy days with flashes of brilliance. The sound of the wind over a grassy hill or through trees traces the landscape elements that colours no longer hold. Some faraway sound, like half-heard fragments of music, becomes snagged on bramble and briar. Blue-grey and green: sky, bare branches, grass, moss. A wren scuttles mouse-like through a labyrinth of branches under a hedge, keeping out of a wind powerful enough to blow it away like a mote of dust. A light snowfall, the first this year, has made far hills sharper and dramatic. The winds have been picking an ancient beech tree apart, limb by limb. From here, the real drama can be seen through the beech and lime boughs above Wenlock Edge. There is a strange pale glow in the plains to the northeast; the floods have returned. The River Severn has burst its banks again and is reclaiming the fields from the mouth of the Severn Gorge at Buildwas, way back into the distance beyond the Welsh border. At least this time of year seems appropriate for floods and the riverlands to reflect the sky with a moody effulgence. All the trickles, brooks and streams move towards the flood, replenished by emphatic rains. Winds blow in from the north, whistling up the changing season.

Winter calls through rooks, frost-clear and dark-edged, even under the filthy mattress stuffing of the sky. From Windmill Hill looking east, a cold wind opens a space for morning and clouds are soaked in pink and yellow. But I am drawn to the west and the woods, to the greyer, darker air which laps against the Edge, where life seems to be lived on a more intimate scale by quick things in shadows.

Breaking cover, crossing the lane and vanishing into a hedge takes the weasel three seconds. Its spine is a whip, propelling it against caution through a hostile, open space where it is exposed. The weasel's life is rapid and secretive. It travels along brambly tunnels and hedgerow byways through wood and field margins, rarely venturing into the open except to kill. Then it drags prey such as rabbit, far larger than itself, back into the anonymity of shadow. The rabbits here look ponderous and slow under the briars, as if they've got 'myxy'. There are tufts of soft grey fur on the path where one has come unstuck, the list of suspects is long.

Fear haunts these woods and many of its inhabitants have good reason to flee when they hear someone coming. A young fallow deer doe runs from the sanctuary of a Lawson's cypress in the remains of a garden, now taken over by the wood. Around the conifer the hopelessly optimistic pink of cyclamen flowers has finally succumbed to frost; the deer only leaves a warm spot on the earth and its scent. Walking between briars and brambles I almost tread on a woodcock which rockets into the air and flares its coppery tail feathers, edged with dark and white bands. I see it for only a few seconds before it vanishes into trees.

There's a moment when the frost still holds and the air is as clear as rook calls. This is when the redwings fly up from Ape Dale making sounds like stones, chaffinch and buntings bound in charms across the field. Then everything hides in the trees while winter comes hunting here, but not with frost this time. What follows is a big wet pig of a day. A day fat with rain, snouting about everywhere, turning everything to muck: the rich brown mole-hills which stood above the frosted ground, the steep clay banks where badgers skid, the Church Green's lawns after Wenlock's Christmas Fair over the weekend. Cold and wet, winter grunts and wild lives take cover.

Still and cold, the sound of passing swan's wings are like fingers rubbed against wet glass. The sun has struggled out of fog a couple of hours before and there is only half an hour of daylight left when the swans go by. The trees have stopped dripping, water thickening with the cold. The last couple of days have been lost in a freezing fog and the landscape is touched by the genius of frost.

This had been an air- not a ground-frost and everything above the green and muddy brown surface of the earth is sugared in rime. Grass stems, hedge twigs, hawthorn berries and tree branches all have a wing of ice along their leeward edges up to 50mm thick. Spider webs look like white plastic. Prickly margins of holly leaves are decorated like something in a Christmas card. Dog rose hips have ice trails like tiny scarlet comets. An Arctic wind has left its aerodynamic signature on every thing that could not move.

Some things are moving. Through the fog, a mixed flock of chaffinch, great- and blue-tits in a tall dense hedge, redwings in hawthorns above the quarry, a mistle thrush in a sweet briar, all move with a quiet secrecy.

The Living Edge – A wanderer's guide to Wenlock Edge • National Trust

A shotgun sounds like a door slamming in the fog far away. Although visibility is down to a couple of hundred metres, less at times, the low sun pierces through for moments of wonder. Then, hedges and groups of trees look as if they are covered in dazzling white blossom. On the dip slope of Wenlock Edge, where the sun did appear, the fields and hedges begin to thaw a little. But in the woods of the scarp slope, a frozen fogbound world persists in a stillness, broken only by a roll of breeze or squirrels chasing through trees, sending a skitter of ice from high branches. Swan-white with a brutal beauty, winter, in case we've forgotten, is the old original superpower.

White and grey, frost and fog, we become an island lost in a sea of murk. Even without any rain for a few weeks, humidity is so high and temperatures so low that a freezing fog settles and refuses to shift. The moods of the fog are strange and remote while at the same time intimate, drawing everything into itself.

The hoar frost rimes grass and trees to create a glassy facsimile of the familiar world which has to be explored anew. The ground is frozen bone-hard which makes traversing the steep wooded slopes of Wenlock Edge easier, but there are no views through the trees; distances deceive, sounds are fugitive. Surrounding hills all but vanished, it seems every footfall finds a new place, even if it falls on somewhere trodden a thousand times before.

Then a storm breaks in during the night and drags the sky away. After days lagged by damp grey cloud, a bright sunny morning with fresh blue skies is a revelation. Suddenly the light is turned on and the landscape reveals itself with the kind of shining confidence not seen for weeks.

This is characterised by a raven, flying in from the west towards the low winter sun, its glossy plumage reflecting the sunlight so that the black bird shines, mirror-silvered, its long wings flashing as they scull across a still blue sky. But the stillness and brightness is not to last. Following the raven comes a wind which strengthens, swinging along the wooded scarp of the Edge, hissing through the grey trunks of ash and the wine-red twigs of lime. Apart from the wind in the canopy, the woods are very quiet. Small birds are being pushed to the leeward edges but other ravens are riding or tacking across the wind. A pair is flying along the Edge making 'kronk-kronk' contact calls through the roar of the wind.

A lone raven flies overhead, sees me and swerves away, then half-turns back to get a better look. We meet at several points over a distance of a few miles. I call to

it. It makes a few cryptic remarks in my direction. I imagine my calls can convey some comradely recognition; a reassurance that I do not carry a gun or any harmful intentions, that I celebrate the mythic status of ravens in this landscape, from which they were purged and during my lifetime have returned in their hundreds. I have to imagine that if the raven's calls represent a piece of its mind, it won't be pretty; there is still illegal persecution. What my kind has done to this landscape is beneath contempt, perhaps we should go back to having battles so it can feast on the slain. From the cliff at Major's Leap, the view across the dale is greying, the wind shifts again.

A new wind blows what little there is left of the old year from the hills. A goldcrest, tiny and olive green with a golden head-stripe, flies nervously through grey light to vanish into ivied shadows like a rumour. The bird appears to embody the shortest day, a last slight feather of a thing to be stripped away before the longest night.

Out of the Winter Solstice comes a new year with a northeasterly running though it; not strong but sharp, scything over the land. Jays in the oak trees, buzzards in the sky; their clear savage notes carry across clear savage air. As the day begins to drain into dark fields and woods, it doesn't seem to matter what numbers are attached to this year or the last, or what date we celebrate the passing from one to another. Whether it's the natural Winter Solstice or the cultural New Years Eve, it's the moments when time seems most fleeting that it has the greatest significance.

As people saunter homeward from their country walks, a lone photographer waits behind his tripod, aiming towards the sunset from Windmill Hill. When would the moment be right to take the picture? What would distinguish the photograph from the moments before and after it? Why would the photograph mean anything without the cold wind, small birds darting into trees and hedges, blackbirds clucking as if alarmed by the impending dusk and the thoughts behind the eye looking into the view finder? Tonight has a story. It is the night when the oak king, the wren, is defeated by the holly king, the robin; a night of symbol and sacrifice but not a story with any purchase on the modern world now. What does it matter? Few people, if any, are about to find out.

Along the edge of the wood, the last of the light catches an ancient beech tree, its great boughs picked apart by storms, the remaining grey trunk and twisted branches glow with cold pale fire. Out in the fields, tall ivied ash trees blacken against the sky, holding firm to their old stories. Through what would be an impenetrable mass of dark branches, a light opens up a space in trees of the hanging woods as the colours of sunset sweep across the sky. The sound of running through leaves vanishes down the steep wooded slope. Is that deer or something else?

The sky overhead is inky blue, fixed by the light of Venus, far brighter than the headlights on the road down below or the few street lamps studding the dark landscape. From the night above the sky fades in lighter bands southwestwards, down to a crimson flame sunset behind the hills far away. Through the layers of colour float black clouds, as if they are the peaks and ridges of a range of higher mountains in another distant, nameless and timeless land, where something else matters.

Geology

By Dr. Peter Toghill

Imagine you are swimming in a warm subtropical sea surrounded by coral reefs. Strange, unfamiliar animals are moving around the reefs, but there are no fish anywhere. Forests of strange starfish-like creatures sway about on the sea bed. But this isn't today, it's 425 million years ago around Wenlock Edge, and we are in the southern tropics near the latitude of present day Tahiti!

Section through the Wenlock Edge area showing cuestas and scarp and vale scenery

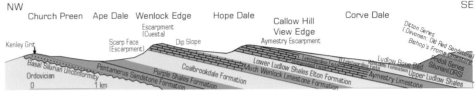

The escarpment of Wenlock Edge, formed by Wenlock Limestone with its famous fossilised coral reefs, is one of the most distinctive features of the Shropshire landscape. In fact, Wenlock Edge is part of a larger type of landscape that covers this part of Shropshire. There are two major escarpments with valleys in between giving rise to a well-known landscape type called Scarp and Vale scenery.

Wenlock Edge is not just an escarpment facing northwest, it also has a more gentle slope to the southeast which geologists call a dip slope. The escarpment and dip slope together give rise to a landform called a cuesta. So really we should call Wenlock Edge a cuesta, not an escarpment, that is just the steep northwest face.

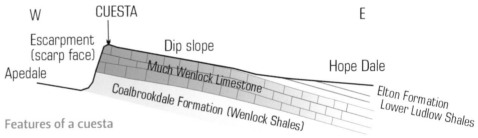

Features of a cuesta

The Wenlock Edge cuesta has been formed by the erosion of alternations of hard and soft layers of sedimentary rocks gently inclined to the southeast by around 10 degrees. The softer rocks (shales and mudstones) form the valleys or dales, the harder rocks (limestones) give rise to the cuestas with their steep escarpments.

Callow Hill, a classic cuesta

The Formation of the rocks of Wenlock Edge

The Silurian Period and Wenlock Edge

The term Silurian, now defined as the period of time between 444 and 416 million years ago, was created by one of the most famous of Victorian geologists Sir Roderick Murchison. In his work on the Silurian System he describes the then little-known rocks of the Welsh Borders, including Shropshire that he found to contain a wonderful variety of fossils. He divided these into a number of small rock divisions and two of these, the Wenlock Series and Ludlow Series, were based on his studies of the rock sequences around these places. These two terms, 'Wenlock' and 'Ludlow', are now internationally recognised subdivisions of the Silurian Period.

Reef limestone at Ippikin's Rock. The red colouration is possibly due to microscopic plants or mineral staining

DEVONIAN Ditton Series (Old Red Sandstone)			St Maughan's Formation Bishops Frome Limestone		**416 Ma**
Pridoli Series (Old Red Sandstone)	No Stages		Raglan Mudstone Formation	450m	
			Temeside Shales Formation	30m	
			Downton Castle Sandstone Formation	12–17m	
			Ludlow Bone Bed	0–15cm	**419 Ma**
Ludlow Series	Ludfordian	Upper Ludlow Shales	Whitcliffe Formation	60–180m	
			Leintwardine Formation	30–200m	
		Aymestry Limestone	Bringewood Formation	60m	
	Gorstian	Lower Ludlow Shales	Elton Formation	120–230m	**423 Ma**
Wenlock Series	Homerian	Wenlock Limestone	Much Wenlock Limestone Formation	21–33m	
		Wenlock Shales	Tickwood Beds (Farley Member)	15–40m	
	Sheinwoodian		Coalbrookdale Formation (Apedale Member)	300m	
			Buildwas Beds	30m	**428Ma**
Llandovery Series	Telychian		Purple Shales Formation	76–107m	
	Aeronian		Pentamerus Sandstone Formation	0–122m	
			Kenley Grit	0–46m	
Major unconformity at base of Silurian					**444 Ma**

Rock types of Wenlock limestone

What is Limestone?

Limestone is a special type of sedimentary rock, one which has been laid down in layers on the sea bed, usually of a warm subtropical sea. Limestone is special because it is made up almost entirely of calcite, the mineral form of the chemical compound calcium carbonate. Limestones can form in two main ways. The calcite can precipitate out of warm subtropical seas which are rich in dissolved calcium carbonate, forming either what are called calcite mudstones, or nodules. The Wenlock Limestone contains nodular limestones and calcite mudstones both of which are called chemical limestones. The second way in which limestones form is by the accumulation of layered masses of the calcite shells of dead sea creatures, such as brachiopods and molluscs; these can be seen forming as shell banks on modern beaches. These limestones are called organic or shell limestones, and are common in the Wenlock Limestone.

A variety of ways of classifying limestones have been developed, the most widely used being based on depositional textures. The terminology can appear rather complicated, so in this account limestones are simply described according to their appearance. Most limestones are pale in colour, although those with a high hydrocarbon content can be almost black. The Wenlock Limestone is usually pale grey to white. Red or brown staining can occur but is usually caused by percolation of iron bearing minerals down from the surface along joint planes, but could be caused by a cover of microscopic plants.

Large calcite vein

Calcite is a grey, white or colourless mineral. It can be confused with quartz but is much softer (hardness 3) compared with the much harder quartz (hardness 7). It is soluble in acid rain water and in the acids produced by car fumes and smoke pollution; hence the problems in many cities where old building are built of limestone. The Wenlock Limestone contains a high percentage of clay and shale beds with no great uninterrupted thicknesses of limestone, so natural caves are not common.

There are two sets of major joints in most sedimentary rocks (but not in fine grained laminated rocks), these are usually at right angles to each other and at right angles to the bedding planes. Joints are caused by expansion when rocks are exposed by erosion. Joints in igneous rocks such as granite and basalt are mainly the result of cooling and shrinking. Limestones can be very pure but often contain small amounts of clay and are then called argillaceous limestones. Although most limestones contain only calcite, secondary mineralisation at a later time can alter the calcite to dolomite, which is calcium magnesium carbonate. This process called dolomitisation has not affected the Wenlock Limestone to any great extent but has often changed the younger Carboniferous Limestone found in northwest Shropshire around Llanymynech Hill. This dolomite rich limestone is very useful as a fertilizer on dairy grasslands.

As the Wenlock Limestone has been buried under younger rocks before erosion exposed it, heat from burial has often reworked the calcite and led to recrystallization in many places, this often destroys the fine structure of fossils. This heat can also lead to the injection of calcite veins often with perfectly formed crystals.

Left: Noticeable on exposed faces of Wenlock Limestone are conspicuous vertical cracks called joints.

Below left: Calcite can form three very different crystal shapes: , sharply pointed crystals called dog tooth spar, crystals with flatter tops called nail head spar, and perfect rhombohedral crystals which when transparent are called Iceland spar. Specimens from Ludlow Museum

Below: Well-formed Iceland spar crystals, commonly sold in mineral shops, show a remarkable physical property of calcite; the ability to split light into two rays by producing double refraction of light and hence polarised light. This is what polaroid sunglasses do but using a manufactured substance.

Variations in the Wenlock limestone

Nodular Limestones

The Wenlock Limestone varies in thickness from around 33 metres in the main area from Ironbridge to Easthope, to around 21 metres near Craven Arms. The majority of the sequence comprises rapid alternations of grey nodular limestone and soft clays and shales. The nodular limestones were formed from chemical precipitates in a warm sea; small nodules grew and eventually joined together to form irregular beds of limestone.

Bentonites

The intervening clays and shales include numerous beds of bentonite up to 10cm thick. Bentonites are clays derived from decayed volcanic ashes and are rich in clay minerals. These minerals, also the main constituents of Fuller's earth, have the property of absorbing large amounts of liquids and then expanding. These bentonite clays are very sticky when wet. When added to eroded normal clays they produce the very sticky muds of Wenlock Edge. Bentonites have in the past caused serious landslips.

Tabular and Crinoidal Limestones

The nodular limestones often pass laterally into thicker beds of more massive crystalline limestone, often recrystallised. Thicker beds form masses with overhangs above thin clay layers and are called tabular limestones. Some of the massive crystalline limestones are made up of shell debris and are thus organic limestones. They are made up of fragments of brachiopods, bryozoans, corals, trilobites and crinoids.

One layer at the very top of the Much Wenlock Limestone is formed almost entirely of crinoid fragments and is called a crinoidal limestone. This weathers to a very distinctive yellow-brown colour; local quarry workers called it the 'Gingerbread bed'. Crinoids (see page 35) are often called sea lilies, but they are in fact stalked echinoderms related to starfish, which attached themselves to the sea bed. The shallow sea bed must have been covered at times with masses of crinoids waving about. Other coarse-grained limestones owe their structure to recrystallisation under the higher temperatures and pressures of later burial.

Below: **Nodular limestone**

Middle: **Bentonites**

Right: **Nodular limestone with bentonite**

Reef Limestones

The most famous type of limestone within the Wenlock Limestone are the reef limestones, often called ballstones.

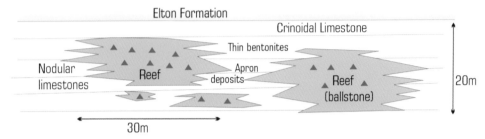

Reef limestones passing laterally into nodular limestones

Many reefs have a layer of bentonite on top of them, as at Knowle Quarry, where ash falls seem to have killed them off.

These were formed in a shallow, clear, warm subtropical sea, probably less than 10 metres deep. The environment was probably similar to areas of the Caribbean today, particularly the Bahama Banks, but in the Southern Hemisphere. By the Middle Silurian Wenlock epoch 425 million years ago, southern Britain had moved north, from near the Antarctic Circle at 500 million years in the Late Cambrian, to 20 degrees south of the equator, a similar latitude to present-day Tahiti.

The reefs are referred to as patch reefs, which grew as individual patches on the shallow sea bed. The reefs have a shape, like a fat discus, and are up to 16 metres thick, although often much thinner than this; they thin in all directions and pass laterally into other types of limestones.

The reefs are massive limestones with no obvious bedding (layering), and are made up of coral, sponge, bryozoan, and crinoid material. The main reef builders are not in fact corals but a type of extinct sponge called stromatoporoids. At many localities, such as Ippikins Rock, the limestones have been recrystallised and the fine structure of fossils has been lost. Nevertheless excellent specimens of corals in position of growth can be found, but many are found broken and upside down which suggest, like modern reefs, that they were subjected to storm damage as they grew near to the surface of the sea.

The reef limestones are common between Ironbridge and Easthope. Around Hilltop and the Wenlock Edge Inn, just west of Easthope, the reefs are at their thickest, up to 16 metres. The famous viewpoint of Ippikins Rock is on top of one of the thickest reefs. Southwest of here, the reef limestones rapidly disappear and are replaced by nodular limestones and shales.

Many of the quarries on Wenlock Edge were first opened on a large scale to obtain pure reef limestones, for use as a flux in the iron furnaces of Coalbrookdale. Locally called ballstones, this was just what was need for ironmaking (see later). Reefs are exposed in all the old quarries from Lilleshall Quarry in the southwest; northeast through Knowle and Lea Quarries, Coates, Ballstone and Edgefield Quarries nearer to Much Wenlock. Farley and Shadwell quarries north of Much Wenlock expose reefs which continue north to the large quarries on Benthall Edge, overlooking the Ironbridge Gorge, with Lincoln Hill quarries just to the north.

A deep cutting west of Much Wenlock where the main A458 road passes to Shrewsbury exposes good reefs above nodular limestones. The cutting was widened in 2008 following a number of landslips. The widened main road from Much Wenlock north to Ironbridge through Farley Dingle exposes limestones of the Farley Member. Further East around Dudley, Much Wenlock Limestone and its reefs come to the surface as steep folds of Silurian rocks within the Coal Measures of the Black Country. Here the reefs and coal seams, together with better iron ore than in Shropshire, provided a base for iron working in the area.

Patch reefs at Coates Quarry, faulted against nodular limestone

Gastropod *Poleumita*

Crinoid *Grissocrinus*

Bryozoan *Thamnopora cristata*

Gastropod *Poleumita*

Brachiopods from Wenlock Limestone

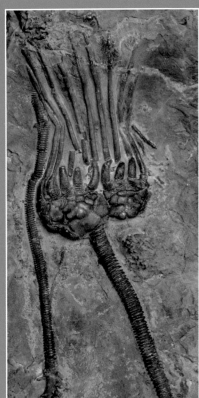

Rugose coral (*Arachnophyllum*)

Halysites coral

Solitary rugose coral (*Omphyma*)

Heliolites coral

Favosites – Tabulate coral

Halysites

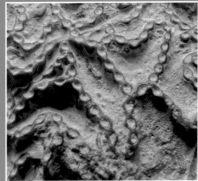

Fossils of Wenlock limestone

The Wenlock Limestone has yielded some beautiful fossils of extinct animals; good examples can be seen in Much Wenlock and Ludlow Museums. Further afield, some of the best Wenlock Limestone fossils are housed in Dudley Museum and the Lapworth Museum of the University of Birmingham Geology Department. One of the great thrills of fossil collecting is to split open a piece of rock and be the first person to set eyes on a creature which has not seen the light of day for millions of years. Much of the fossil material occurs around the edge of the reefs in what are called reef apron deposits. Being formed in shallow water the reefs were subjected to storm damage; many corals and other animals were broken up and washed to the sides and margins of the reefs before being fossilised. Many lumps of limestone contain a great mixture of fossil debris, corals are often found upside down having been broken off the reef and washed about during storms.

Responsible collecting: There is little point in hammering rock faces to extract fossils, anyway this is not allowed on National Trust land. The best specimens are found where the rock has naturally weathered to reveal the fossils in scree slopes. Be aware of National Trust regulations on fossil collecting, and always seek permission to collect on private land. Good and unusual specimens should be offered to local museums.

Corals: The Wenlock Limestone contains numerous patch reefs, described above, which have been built up mainly by corals and sponges. The corals belong to two main groups, now extinct, the rugose and tabulate corals. Rugose corals can be solitary or joined together, tabulate corals are colonial. Many of the most well known Wenlock Limestone corals are tabulate forms, including favosites, halysites and heliolites.

Sponges: Large layered structures looking like fossil cabbages, are in fact ancient fossil calcareous sponges called stromatoporoids.

Crinoids: These still live today and can be likened to starfish attached to the sea bed by a stalk. When waving about on the sea bed they do look a bit plant-like. The arms, initially five, keep splitting, so the creature can end up with many arms waving about in the water attracting food particles to its mouth. Whole fossilised crinoids are rare, but when found are very beautiful; more often just the segments of the stems are found.

Bryozoans: Bryozoans are marine many-celled colonial animals which secrete a calcareous skeleton. They live today and include branching 'sea mosses' and encrusting 'sea mats'. They are common in Wenlock Limestone forms as both branching and encrusting forms.

Trilobites: These are not particularly common in the Wenlock Limestone of Wenlock Edge but more common in the same limestone around Dudley.

Brachiopods: These marine creatures with two shells were very common in the past but rare today. They are abundant in the Wenlock Limestone and probably lived around the edges of the reefs.

Gastropods: Marine 'snails' are often found in the limestone and confused with ammonites, which are only from much younger strata, mainly Jurassic.

Stromatoporoids

Clematocrinus Crinoid

Trilobite

Knowle Quarry fault plane

Formation of Wenlock Edge as a landform

Many geological processes have taken place to form the famous landform of Wenlock Edge since its limestones were formed in shallow subtropical seas, on the other side of the world, around 425 million years ago. The area was buried for nearly 400 million years until around 30 million years ago when the present landscape started to emerge. After the limestones had formed on the sea bed the area was buried under further sediments and rocks. The rocks of the Wenlock Edge area, still buried under later sediments, were folded and the layers inclined at an angle similar to today. Fractures, called faults, were also produced during periods of earth movements, and rocks displaced either side of the fault plane by a few centimeters or many metres. Striated and polished surfaces, called 'slikensides' often occur on exposed fault planes and can be covered with crystals, as at Knowle Quarry fault plane.

About 65 million years ago, an event happened which was to start the shaping of the present day British landscape. At this time the north and west of Britain was raised up and tilted to the southeast; the buried Wenlock Edge rocks were further tilted to the southeast. As erosion got to work on the new land surface around 50 million years ago, many thousands of metres of younger rocks were stripped away to expose older rocks in north and west Britain, including Shropshire. By around 20 million years ago the shapes of the Shropshire Hills had started to appear; the Silurian rocks of Wenlock Edge were exposed for the first time since their formation over 400 million years ago.

During the period 65 million years to around 2 million years ago, (the Tertiary period) the landscape of Britain took shape. Earth movements took place over Shropshire which produced movements along new and old fault planes. A number of faults displaced the rocks on Wenlock Edge, notably around Hill Top and Roman Bank. One of the most spectacular movements was along the Church Stretton Fault where rocks were pushed down on the western side of the fault by 1000 metres. This has resulted in Wenlock Limestone and other Silurian rocks being found in the bottom of the Stretton valley and on the western slopes of Caer Caradoc.

Wenlock Edge during the Ice Age

Around 2 million years ago major ice sheets started to form over highland Britain and spread south and east. This is the Quaternary Period, the one that we are still living in today. The Ice Age finished around 10,000 years ago, but as recently as 20,000 years ago an ice sheet up to 300 metres thick covered north Shropshire and spread south to the flanks of the South Shropshire Hills. The higher Shropshire hills probably stood above the ice but parts of Wenlock Edge escarpment were overridden by tongues of ice. The landscape was not physically worn away by it, in fact the main effects came from the melt waters during the retreat phase starting 17,000 years ago when sands and gravels (some brought from further north), were deposited in valley bottoms.

Some areas around Wenlock Edge are covered with a thin layer of glacial boulder clay; a sticky clay full of boulders (called erratics) derived from elsewhere, then left behind when the ice melts. Although most of the boulder clay is found in Ape Dale, areas of Hope Dale and the dip-slope of the Aymestry Limestone are covered with this clay. It is very acidic and gives rise to acid soils on limestones. Quarrying at Lea South Quarry, on the dip slope of Wenlock Edge and into Hope Dale, has exposed glacial boulder clays (called tills) overlying Elton Formation beds. The boulder clays contain granite erratics from Scotland and also local rocks from Ape Dale such as Pentamerus Beds.

One major event during the Ice Age affected the northern areas of Wenlock Edge; the formation of the Ironbridge Gorge. Prior to the Ice Age the river Severn flowed north from Welshpool to the Dee estuary. When ice sheets blocked this route, the river produced a deep channel under the ice flowing east (a subglacial channel). Water under pressure cut through the then continuous Wenlock Edge escarpment to form the Ironbridge Gorge. This left one small piece of Wenlock Limestone north of the gorge which today forms Lincoln Hill. Since the ice sheets finally left Shropshire around 10,000 years ago, the processes of erosion (rain, snow and wind), have continued to eat away at the escarpments which will continue to retreat slowly southeast, until new geological events take over.

Quarrying and uses of limestone

For many hundreds of years, limestone on Wenlock Edge has been quarried for a variety of uses: building stone, aggregate, lime for agriculture, lime mortar, and as a constituent in the iron making industries of the Ironbridge area.

Building Stone: The Wenlock Limestone, particularly the tabular and nodular forms, has been used extensively in the local area but is not a high quality stone. It is difficult to cut into smooth sided blocks but does usually possess one or two smooth joint surfaces for use as facings to walls. Better quality sandstones are used for doorways and windows. As a limestone it is prone to weathering by acid rain.

Lime and Lime Mortar: A good deal of limestone has been extracted in the past for burning, to make quick lime for agriculture and slaked lime for lime mortar. Wenlock Limestone has a relatively low magnesium content so is not as useful for agriculture.

Iron Making: Wenlock Limestone played a vital role in iron making in the Industrial Revolution in nearby Coalbrookdale and the Ironbridge area. The local iron ore of the Ironbridge area is called a clay ironstone. It occurs mainly as irregular lumps or nodules made of iron carbonate but with a high content of clay impurity. If pure limestone is added as a flux to the mix of iron ore and coke, the limestone reacts with the clay impurities to form a blue-green glassy basic slag, this floats to the top of the melt and can be siphoned off. This process is called fluxing. The slag was used extensively as a ballast between the lines on railway tracks throughout the region. Along the lines of may old disused railway tracks in Shropshire you will find lumps of this pretty blue green glassy slag looking a bit like lava, often with gas bubble holes.

Furnace slag

For this process only the pure reef limestones can be used, many of the older quarries of Wenlock Edge were opened up or enlarged during the 19th century. The new railway from Ironbridge to Much Wenlock was initially extended southwest in the 19th century to serve Knowle, Lea and Lilleshall quarries.

Quarrying techniques: On the main part of Wenlock Edge, southwest of Much Wenlock, quarrying has taken place on the dip slope to the west of the road to Church Stretton. This dip-slope area, including Knowle,

Quarrying on Wenlock Edge

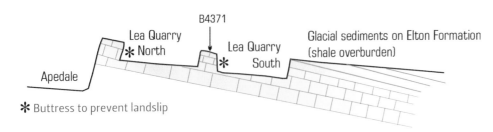

* Buttress to prevent landslip

Lea, Coates, Ballstone and Lilleshall quarries, was also convenient in the late 19th century, being close to the developing railway. The problem here is that quarrying has sometimes gone right up to the edge of the escarpment, leaving large faces overlooking the quarries with the rock layers dipping into the quarry. Where sticky bentonite clay bands occurred, this led to large landslips forming along glide planes inclined into the quarries. After 1973 the quarrying companies were instructed to build buttresses up against used faces to prevent landslips.

In recent years the dip-slope area southeast of the Much Wenlock to Church Stretton road has been developed and extended into Lilleshall Quarry. Here, an overburden of shales made extraction more difficult. All the quarries listed above were exploited for the pure reefs in the 19th century, mainly for the iron furnaces of the Coalbrookdale area. Since 1950 stone from the quarries on Wenlock Edge has been mainly exploited for aggregate.

Lea South Quarry, 2010

FURTHER READING

Toghill, P. *Geology of Shropshire*, 2nd edition, Crowood Press, 2006.

Toghill, P. *Geology of Britain*, Crowood Press, 2000.

Archaeology & Landscape History

By Dr. Ian Dormor

Seen from the air, Wenlock Edge stands out as the major feature of the South Shropshire landscape; a limestone ridge running some 20 miles from Much Wenlock to Craven Arms. Whilst the ridge, more properly described as an escarpment or a *cuesta* in today's scientific terminology, is a natural feature of considerable scientific and environmental importance, it has a fascinating archaeology and landscape history stretching back some 5000 years or more.

Blakeway Hollow is a fine
example of a hollow way

The Landscape Framework

Wenlock Edge lies at the core of a range of linear hill ridges whose northeast/southwest orientation provides a distinct topographical trend to this part of South Shropshire. Even today, as in the past, these hill ridges present an obstacle to travel, making east-west journeys far more complicated than north-south ones. This factor alone has contributed to the relative isolation of the localities to the west of the Edge and over towards Wales.

The Edge forms a natural division between two locally distinctive areas; Ape Dale to the west and Hope Dale to east of the ridge. This division has determined the layout and orientation of many parish, estate and property boundaries whose origins have a long history extending back into the mists of time.

Rocks and routeways

Above all, it is the geology of Wenlock Edge that has created this distinctive landscape. For the past 50 years, it has been recognised as being of national importance, designated as part of the Shropshire Hills Area of Outstanding Natural Beauty (AONB).

The geology chapter of this book explains how Wenlock Edge, a limestone escarpment of great renown, was formed. That limestone, which gave rise to a major local industry, provided, by its relative hardness, an obstacle to the natural forces of erosion more successfully than the softer rocks of the intervening dales. It also provided the focus of the local economy and a vital means of communication as a natural routeway through the undulating hill-and-dale landscape. As such, the Edge has, for millennia, provided the platform for what was and still is, the principal route connecting the Severn Valley with the Shropshire Hills and Wales; a road that became part of an ancient network of routes that connected such diverse places as Bristol, Chester, London and Shrewsbury. The strategic nature of this route along the Edge was later mirrored with the construction of a railway line that ran from Craven Arms to Wellington.

In this journey through history, we will look at features that have been created by the activities of people, animals and machines over many centuries. These features, which range from earthworks, boundaries, tracks, hollow ways, quarries and buildings, provide the evidence by which we can reconstruct the landscape history and archaeology of Wenlock Edge; they are the tangible remains of interaction by human beings with the natural landscape over time. This physical evidence is supported by place-names, which provide indications of the origins and dates of settlements, and maps which provide a graphic insight into landscapes of the past, now hidden within the contemporary landscape. It is by combining these different forms of evidence that we can reconstruct landscapes at different periods, detecting the evolutionary processes that have contributed to the way the landscape appears today. As you get your 'eye' in, you will find that experience gained from an exploration of Wenlock Edge will enable you to look at landscapes elsewhere and unravel the mysteries they hold.

These different strands of evidence complement each other; none need be taken in isolation. If you study the map and see a strange feature, such as a road that goes nowhere or a peculiar kink in a boundary, look at some old maps to see whether there is a ready explanation. Perhaps the road terminated at a village, long deserted, or the boundary resulted from a former wood that has long disappeared. These features remain as 'ghosts' of past landscapes in the landscape of today; clues for the landscape detective to unravel.

Woods and tracks

The major feature of Wenlock Edge is the woodland, much of which has been managed for centuries by coppicing. Most of our native broadleaved trees have the capacity to regenerate from cut stumps, this feature has been exploited by man since Neolithic times, (about 5000 years ago) as a way of obtaining a continuous supply of small poles and small wood for making artefacts and wood for fuel. The woods were a resource used by people who lived in settlements strung out along the length of Wenlock Edge. Their routes into the woods and between settlements remain as old tracks. Some of these also originated as routes taken to and from work by men working in the stone and limestone quarries on the Edge. On the Edge, a very common feature is the sunken lane, or hollow way; nowadays a footpath, but in past times a highway, created by the passage of countless hooves, feet and cart wheels. They are usually found where trackways ascend slopes. The wear and tear of all that traffic upon soft rocks over time caused the tracks to be cut down and hollowed out. In Blakeway Hollow, one of the main routes on to the Edge from Much Wenlock, you can still see the grooves formed by wagon wheels; a lasting reminder of the past.

The most widespread type of earthwork feature you might come across is the sinuous low bank, which occurs in many woods. Many of these banks are 'woodbanks'; the remains of hedge banks that once surrounded blocks of woodland. They could also be boundary banks, setting out the alignment of parish or property

Donkey at Ballstone Quarry, Blakeway Hollow

boundaries, many of which are still in use today; look at the modern map and see if your bank coincides with the parish boundary. The 1:25000 Explorer map is particularly good for this.

The extractive industries on Wenlock Edge, primarily based upon the limestone, have created many features, big and small. Some small, long abandoned quarries now remain as holes in the hillside, whereas the more recent quarrying of the Edge has created huge voids, a number of which are filling with water. Another common feature that remains hidden in the woods originated from the making of charcoal. You may come across pits that were used for sawing wood, now remaining as depressions in the ground. But the most common feature is the charcoal hearth or pitstead; a flattened area where charcoal burning once took place. It is usually possible to find these features from spreads of black soil on the woodland floor; the remains of charcoal production.

Place-names

These are the common forms of physical evidence one might encounter on an exploration of Wenlock Edge. There is, however, another, perhaps more cryptic form of evidence in the names of places on and around the Edge. It is an interesting exercise to take a map of the area and highlight all the places with names ending in -ley, -hop(e) or -ton. These suffixes are an indication of settlements that probably originated in the Anglo-Saxon period, twelve centuries ago.

The distinctive vernacular buildings of south Shropshire are a reflection of the use of local materials; stone for the ground floor elevations with timber framing above and stone slates for the roof. A number of these remain on and around the Edge; an almost 'organic' form of resource use. Brick buildings are rarely as old as the stone versions and the use of local stone for building is a good guide to finding out how old a building might be.

In summary, Wenlock Edge may be seen as a major element of the physical landscape of south Shropshire; the longest wooded escarpment in Britain and a natural feature which provided a framework and basis for settlement, communication and industry over many centuries. The Edge contains much of interest for both the casual enquirer or the more serious researcher, for it is quite probable that there are still features that remain to be identified by the inquisitive walker or visitor to the area. This chapter now moves to provide an historical background into which these physical features may be set.

Wenlock Edge – Prehistoric

Although hill ridges have long been thought to have had a particular prominence as routeways used by prehistoric people, scant evidence for human activity on Wenlock Edge before the Iron Age has been found to date. This is not to say that there was no prehistoric activity here; more that nothing obvious has come to light in the absence of focused research. The traditional, now somewhat discredited, view is that hill ridges provided easy routes through the landscape as opposed to valleys choked by trees and vegetation.

The evidence

The most tangible evidence for prehistoric activity on Wenlock Edge is in the form of an Iron Age hillfort called Larden Ditches in Mogg Forest, near to Wilderhope Manor. Another indication of Iron Age occupation in the Wenlock Edge area comes from a possible Iron Age farm at Stanway.

Larden Ditches is the major prehistoric feature of Wenlock Edge, having defences that are comparable in size to some of the larger hillforts along the Welsh Marches. Hillforts are thought to have been occupied as permanent settlements rather than places of refuge where communities could shelter in times of strife. Covering nearly six hectares, Larden Ditches is circular in shape, and surrounded by three ditches. It is accessible from a public footpath and well worth a visit.

Whilst no other indications of human activity during the Neolithic and Bronze Age have been found to date on Wenlock Edge, it is always possible that evidence will come to light in the future, for Neolithic tools have been found not far away, on high ground west of Shipton. At Brockton, towards the Ditches, a Bronze Age cremation burial has been identified. There is considerable evidence for human activity in the wider Wenlock Edge area during the Iron Age. A number of ditched enclosures have been located on the northwestern ridge near to the Wenlock-Ludlow road and sherds of Romano-British pottery have been found at the Ditches and elsewhere.

The Romano-British Period

As with early prehistory, there is little tangible evidence of the Romans on Wenlock Edge, perhaps somewhat surprising considering that the area lay within the hinterland of Wroxeter, the fourth largest city in Britain during the Roman period. It seems probable that the Iron Age way of life continued here despite the Romans and that the established practices of settlement and land-use did not change with their coming. The county of Shropshire is not populated with a high density of Roman villas in the way that, for example, Gloucestershire is. Roman settlement is evident at Harley, near Much

Wenlock, where local schoolteacher W. A. Silvester conducted excavations on a villa site between 1956 and 1962. Two other villas are known in the vicinity of Wenlock Edge at Rushbury and Acton Scott, where excavations took place in 2008 and 2009 to reassess the extent of the archaeology, first uncovered in the 1840s by Mrs Frances Stackhouse Acton.

Fields and farmsteads

It seems possible, indeed probable, that the field layout of some of parishes whose boundaries abut the Edge originated in the Iron Age; such is the evidence indicated by the crop marks of Iron Age farms seen on aerial photographs. Elsewhere on Wenlock Edge, it is thought likely that Romanisation brought in a reorganisation of the prehistoric field patterns, using the Edge as a boundary in the creation of estates during the 4th century. Certainly agriculture would have had a major role during the Romano-British period, with a large and ready market close by at Wroxeter, where five thousand people are thought to have lived.

We can envisage the form and function of these small Romano-British farms from evidence found elsewhere in Britain, where the common form of domestic building is the thatched round house; a continuation of Iron Age practice. Sites of the period having rectangular rather than round buildings are thought to show evidence of the local populace seeking to emulate the Roman lifestyle with more substantial buildings.

Evidence of activity during the Romano-British period is somewhat more convincing at nearby Much Wenlock, where it is thought from recent excavations that a Roman building stood on the site later occupied by the Medieval priory. It was originally thought that the building was a disused villa, whose standing walls attracted the 7th

Wenlock Priory

century monastery builders to choose the site for their foundation, but this theory has been challenged.

In 1983 a group of burials dated to the post-Roman period was discovered in the town behind a house in Barrow Street. Nearer to Wenlock Edge, at Stretton Westwood, there was discovered in 1977 a hoard of almost 2000 coins, mostly dating from the late 3rd century and the 4th century.

The Wroxeter hinterland

The excavation evidence from Wroxeter has demonstrated that cattle, rather than sheep formed the basis of the town's economic base. Given the close proximity of the farmsteads established along the margins of the Edge, it follows that pastoral farming probably formed the basis of the rural economy from the 3rd to 6th centuries AD, with Wroxeter sourcing much of its requirement for meat and hides from the nearby rural hinterland.

With the withdrawal of the Roman army from Britain in the 4th century, Wroxeter seems to have become the focus of a tribal chiefdom until the 6th century, when it gradually began to lose its importance as an administrative centre in favour of Shrewsbury. At this stage Britain entered what used to be referred to as the Dark Ages, but nowadays, the Post-Roman and Anglo-Saxon period.

Post-Roman and Anglo-Saxon

The Post-Roman and Anglo-Saxon period had a particular significance for Wenlock Edge, principally due to the founding, in AD680, of St Milburga's convent at Much Wenlock. It is apparent from archaeological evidence that Wroxeter remained occupied until well into the 6th century AD, and that British communities survived in the region alongside their Anglo-Saxon rulers. Milburga, abbess of Much Wenlock Priory, was the granddaughter of Penda, the founder of the kingdom of Mercia. Penda had installed his son (her father Merewalh), as head of the Anglo-Saxon tribe known as the Magonsaete. Their tribal lands were extensive, covering much of Herefordshire and south Shropshire including the Corve Dale as far north as Much Wenlock.

It is apparent that the Priory was flourishing at the beginning of the 10th century, for it is mentioned in a charter dated AD901 bestowing a grant of land and a gold chalice in honour of Abbess Milburga, before the Priory is reputed to have been destroyed by the Vikings. It is evident in the place-names of a number of villages near to Wenlock Edge, that settlements were being established there in the Anglo-Saxon period. Particularly significant are those place-names ending in -ley, which indicate the creation of settlements out of woodland clearings.

This place-name suffix provides an indication of the extent of woodland on Wenlock Edge in the early Medieval period; it is known to have come into common use in Shropshire between AD750 to AD950. A band of 'forest clearings' can be seen running east/west through the centre of Shropshire, although it may be that some settlements were only so named as late as the 10th century when the word was beginning to lose its original meaning and refer more to 'pasture' than 'woodland'. This appears to have been the case at Hughley, which did not originate until the 12th century through a grant of land to Sir Hugh de Lega, whose family later took the name of Lee.

Another characteristic place-name, which is fairly common on and around Wenlock Edge, is that which ends in –hope, an element that is locally associated with places situated in secluded valleys. In Hope Dale, which lies between the Edge and the Aymestrey Limestone Escarpment that faces the Corve Dale, there are a number of places with the –hope element. It is thought that these places were established, permanently occupied hamlets, rather than more temporary settlements that shifted over time along the valley.

The early Medieval woods

During the early Medieval period, and for many centuries thereafter, woodland was of huge significance to the human population as a critical resource whose importance was second only to food. Whilst woodland provided raw materials and fuel, it was also of major importance as a resource for grazing animals. It is thought that much of the woodland during the Anglo-Saxon period was managed as wood pasture; a dual-purpose system of growing wood on pollarded trees that were situated in open grassland. Here poles could be harvested from trees growing on grazed grassland. Under the feudal system, peasant communities had to exploit wooded commons for their needs, for both wood and for grazing, as the principal stands of woodland were invariably the property of their seigneurial masters.

Much of our knowledge of woodland and its management stems from the records kept by manor courts, of punishments handed down to people who had the misfortune of being caught taking wood without permission, or allowing their animals to graze in woods where grazing was forbidden. A quite common crime was that of hedge-breaking; removal of dead hedges

from coppice woods to provide fuel for cooking and heating. In some cases the punishments could be very severe, with prison or beatings for repeat offenders, as opposed to the rather more commonplace fines levied for merely stealing wood.

Field boundaries

When looking at the layout of the countryside and its administrative boundaries, it is evident that Wenlock Edge has been the major landscape feature to which many parish boundaries are related. It is apparent that the boundaries of Saxon estates, and the prehistoric field patterns that preceded them, used the Edge as a collective boundary, not least because the woodland that clothed the western face was regarded as a common good and consequently each estate, manor or township had a share in it.

Easthope is of particular interest in that the parish straddles the Edge and two different forms of field boundary enclosure patterns are visible on either side of the Edge. On the eastern side the Medieval open fields ran up to the crest of the Edge. These open fields were enclosed by agreement in the Tudor period (piecemeal enclosure). Today they appear quite different from the fields on the western side of the Edge; smaller, irregular fields which originated as assarts (Medieval woodland clearances to create farmland).

Generally the parishes on the western side of Wenlock Edge, e.g. Harley, Hughley and Eaton extended between the crest of the Edge and the springline at the Edge foot. The Edge formed the western boundary of Presthope, in Hope Dale, which had little woodland in comparison with the Ape Dale parishes, hence its field pattern is far more regular, albeit formed from the piecemeal enclosure of the open fields.

Sign to Easthope at Hilltop
(by Wenlock Edge Inn)

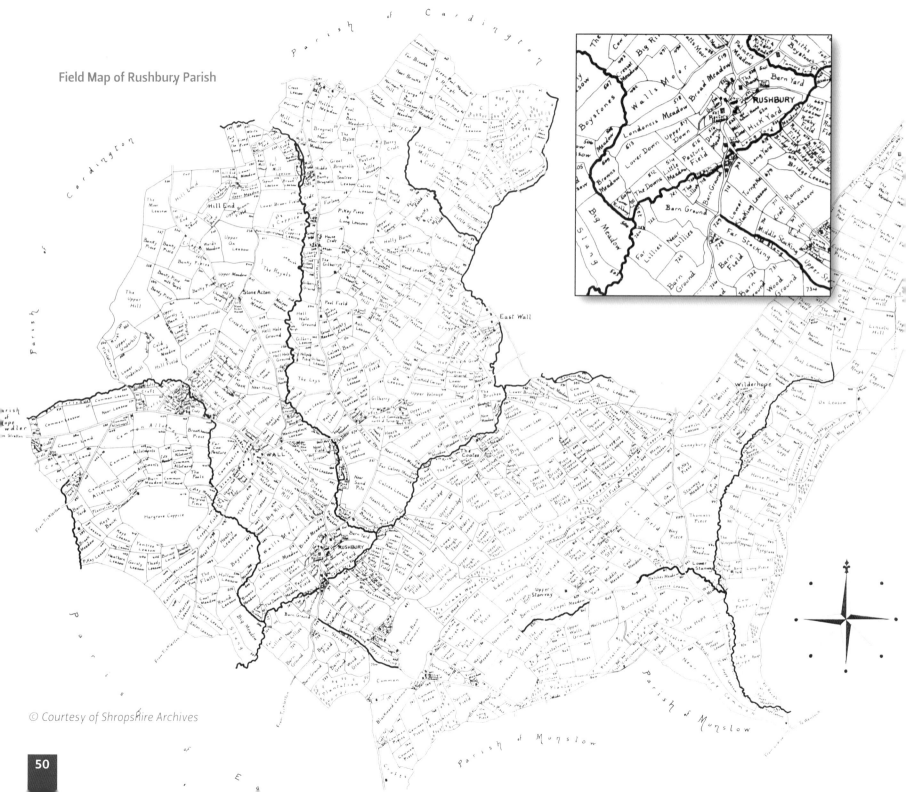

Field Map of Rushbury Parish

© Courtesy of Shropshire Archives

The field pattern today is altered considerably from that of 150 years ago when the Tithe maps were drawn up. It is an interesting exercise to contrast the field pattern of the 1840s with that of today to see how much has changed. Fieldname maps provide a snapshot of a time when the Medieval field patterns could still be discerned from the 19th century boundaries and the distinctive names that were given to the fields. These can be inspected at Shropshire Archives (or on the website www.secretshropshire.org.uk).

Post Conquest – Medieval

Shortly after the Norman Conquest of AD1066, great areas of the English countryside became royal forests where the prime concern was the care of the King's deer. Indeed the term 'forest' refers not to a landscape thickly set with trees but is a legal term. This was an area where forest was imposed to protect the deer and their habitat. Wenlock Edge lay within the Long Forest, which stretched from Craven Arms to Buildwas and took in the Long Mynd and the Stretton Hills. Wenlock Edge formed the spine of the forest and its name reflects the inclusion of the Edge within its bounds.

Domesday, that first great survey of the English countryside which took place in AD1086 by order of William the Conqueror, mentions a number of the settlements along the margins of Wenlock Edge such as Ticklerton, Stanway and Rushbury. It gives an impression of a busy wooded countryside dotted with small villages not unlike that which we see today. The entry for Ticklerton describes the woodland as being sufficient to fatten 60 pigs. Just a small place, there were only six villagers, six smallholders and one rider with five ploughs. Stanway was even smaller, having three villagers and one smallholder with two ploughs. There

is no mention of woodland there although it is unlikely that none existed. Rushbury had a mill, a hawk's eyrie and woodland sufficient for fattening 40 pigs.

Forest Law

Under forest law, quite horrendous punishments could be handed down to those unfortunate to be caught poaching deer, cutting wood or allowing their animals to graze in prohibited areas. Royal forests were not uninhabited areas, many were populated with villages whose inhabitants had to try and lead normal lives, growing crops and working in the fields in a situation where their efforts could be trashed by hunting parties in hot pursuit of the chase, without recourse to compensation. This situation changed for the better after the disforestation of the Long Forest in 1301. There is a reminder of those days at Upper Millichope, where the 12th century house of the King's Forester (which also served as a jail) remains as part of a farm complex.

From the earliest times there was a tension between areas of woodland and the need to extend the amount of land where arable crops could be cultivated to feed a growing population in the 12th and 13th centuries. Small areas of woodland were cleared to form new fields, a process called assarting. Often, permission to assart was agreed with the payment of a sum of money but there were occasions when it was done illegally. We know of instances where people were prosecuted through surviving documentary evidence. Typically, a person named Parnel of Kenley was fined for making an assart into the forest at Wilderhope in 1250.

This period was of great significance for Wenlock Edge due to the influence of Wenlock Abbey upon the town and its rural hinterland. The foundation in AD1079–82 of a Cluniac monastery at Much Wenlock by Roger de Montgomery saw the incorporation of a large tract of south Shropshire into the abbey's estate. The priory lands embraced most of the parishes of Much Wenlock, Broseley, Little Wenlock, Madeley and those parts of the manors of Harley and Hughley east of the Hughley Brook. Land was also held at Longville, Ditton Priors, Eaton and Stoke St Milborough. Effectively, almost the entire length of Wenlock Edge fell within the boundary of Much Wenlock, and therefore was subject to the laws and taxes imposed by the Priory. This meant that all the woodland on Wenlock Edge came under the ownership of the Priory until the abbey was dissolved in 1540. Overall the extent of the monastic estate was some 9,000 acres.

Commons

For the Medieval landless peasant, commons were a vital resource where animals could be grazed, peat could be dug and wood could be gathered. Contrary to popular belief, commons were, and are still, not a free-for-all. They are always owned by someone, and during the Medieval period this would have been the lord of the manor. People, who were authorised to utilise the resources of the common, held common rights. Today these rights are vested in properties rather than individuals, but in the Medieval period they would have been afforded to village residents by the lord of the manor. Common rights have strange names that persist to the present day. For example, the right of *estovers* gave the commoner the legal right to take firewood (as opposed to timber) from the common. The right of *piscary* enabled the commoner to fish in pools on the common, and the right of *hedgebote* enabled commoners to take wood from the common to repair the hedges around their cottages. One common right, which was particularly pertinent to Wenlock Edge, was

the right of *pannage*. This strange word means the release of pigs into woodland during the autumn to eat acorns and beech mast. Interestingly in some instances, Domesday Book describes the extent of manorial woodland in terms of the numbers of pigs that can be accommodated rather than their areas.

Coppicing the trees

A very common earthwork feature you might come across in the woodlands on Wenlock Edge is a woodbank. These linear features, sometimes with trees or old hedges growing out of them, are the earthwork relics of former coppice hedgebanks. Woodbanks are particularly evident in Blakeway Coppice, Holly Coppy and Easthope Wood. They are the remains of hedge banks which divided up areas of woodland into distinct compartments. Prior to the introduction of fossil fuels such as coal and oil in the 18th and 19th centuries, wood was the second most important commodity to food and, because of this, it was conserved and managed by coppicing in order to secure a continuous and sustainable supply. The physical act of coppicing involves cutting a tree down to almost ground level and leaving a stump (or stool) in place. New wood arises very quickly from the stool as a profusion of stems. The time span between coppicing events is determined by the size of wood required. If the main requirement was poles and sticks, the coppice cycle might be as short as 8–10 years. For larger sized stems, for fencing, charcoal making and firewood, it might be as long as 15–25 years, depending on the location of the woodland and the tree species involved. The coppiced wood was often referred to as 'underwood'.

Timber trees, those that were allowed to grow naturally as 'maiden' trees to maturity for constructional timber, were called 'standards' or 'overwood'. After the trees were coppiced it was vital to exclude grazing animals such as cattle, sheep, horses, goats and particularly deer from the regenerating stools as the animals found the young shoots very appetising. The usual way of doing this was to surround the area of cut coppice with a 'dead' hedge, usually made from branches of prickly species such Hawthorn, Blackthorn and Crab Apple. The coppice hedges (sometimes called fences) were usually set on banks, woodbanks, like those which can be seen today in the woods on Wenlock Edge. Many woods that have been managed since Medieval times preserve their woodbanks today. They are not always clearly visible; the winter is often the best time to see them when they are not obscured by vegetation. It is highly likely that many of the woodbanks you might come across whilst walking in woodland on the Edge originated in Medieval times.

Below: **A coppice stool**
Right: **Hazel poles cut for hedge laying**

The old trees tell of past management

Whilst coppice was the customary method of managing woodland during the later Middle Ages and until as recently as the early 19th century, a much earlier form of woodland management called 'wood pasture' was commonplace at the time of Domesday Book. Originating in the Anglo-Saxon period, wood pasture provided a means of combining grazing with wood production. This was achieved by pollarding the trees so that the re-growing shoots emerged at a height above the reach of grazing animals; it was in effect, 'coppicing on a stick'. The effect of both coppicing and pollarding is to extend the normal lifespan of broadleaved trees and therefore you will find that many of our oldest 'veteran' trees are old pollards. Their trunks have a distinctive goblet shape, with the limbs emerging from an old pruning surface, which is particularly evident during the winter months when the trees are free of foliage. Coppiced stools, which have been left uncut for over 50 years, begin to revert to mature trees but with the distinction of having more than one main stem. If you find a tree with two or more stems growing out of what appears to be a common trunk, it will invariably have been coppiced at some time. If you come across a large number of such trees in a small area, you will have discovered an area of old coppice.

Coppiced tree near Oldfield Coppice

The black art of charcoal burning

The Wenlock Edge woodlands were coppiced for centuries to provide the raw materials for charcoal burning. Charcoal is an ancient fuel. It is carbonised wood, whose moisture content has been reduced to zero by a process of incomplete combustion. As a result charcoal has a very high calorific value and was in demand for smelting ores and other industrial processes. There was great demand locally from limeburners who used charcoal for firing their kilns before coal became available with the advent of the railway. Much locally-produced charcoal was used just over the border at Bringewood in Herefordshire where there was a large iron works. Such was the intensity of this once commonplace rural industry on Wenlock Edge, that the woods are today populated by numerous charcoal-burning sites and the ancillary works that went with the process. Hence there are platforms for stacking wood, the coppice woods themselves, saw pits, charcoal hearths, or pitsteads, where you can still find copious amounts of very dark or black soil, and the trackways which were used to take the finished product to its point of use. The woodlands then contain the archaeological evidence of a major industry which has largely disappeared from view. Whilst some limekilns remain in various stages of disintegration, the trees, earthworks and trackways persist as silent reminders of a time when the woods were full of people making things, cutting the coppices, carting wood, making charcoal and taking the end product away.

Top left: **Charcoal burning from Evelyn's *'Silva'* 1664**
Top right: **Coppiced wood stems form the core of a charcoal clamp**
Bottom right: **Newly-made charcoal**

that they tend to have sinuous boundaries, typically a reversed-S shape still preserved in the hedgelines, originated through the process of ploughing with a team of oxen. In order to turn the plough team in sufficient time to not to have to reverse the animals at the end of the furrow, it was normal practice to turn the team well before they reached the end of the field. This gradual turning process created the characteristic boundaries that can still be seen in many parts of the country, including Shropshire.

Another development, which led to the retention of the reversed-S field shape in the hedgelines, was the process of Piecemeal Enclosure which began in Shropshire as early as the late 15th century. This was in effect a redesign of the countryside following the abandonment of the open field system and a move towards tenant and yeomen farming. The process of Piecemeal Enclosure resulted in the amalgamation of the open field strips into larger combinations of land which were usually hedged, (almost the same process as someone purchasing part of his neighbour's garden and placing a hedge around the resulting larger plot). Invariably the hedges that resulted from Piecemeal Enclosure, where they have been retained, frequently indicate that the land was formerly an open field.

Post Medieval – Early Modern

Roads old and new
Wenlock Edge has provided a strategic route through south Shropshire for millennia. While there is no tangible evidence of prehistoric trading, the existence of this natural route through the hills must have provided a means of access between the Severn valley and the Onny and Clun catchments.

Look at the hedges
The people who worked in the woods lived in the local settlements that fringe Wenlock Edge. A number of these are thought to have originated in the early Medieval period under the auspices of Wenlock Abbey. It is still possible to pick out the outlines of the open fields associated with these settlements, for they remain fossilised into the network of field boundaries that have come and gone over time. Open field agriculture was a feature of the Medieval countryside, where typically three fields, which were lotted up into strips, were farmed in rotation. Each villager had a number of strips allocated in each field which were cultivated to provide sustenance for his family. He was also required to work on the manorial land under the feudal system. A characteristic of open fields is

The road across Wenlock Edge, which linked Much Wenlock with Church Stretton, was turnpiked between 1765 and 1867, becoming an established main road in 1889. The road from Hughley to Harley, depicted on a map dated 1769, ran through Blakeway holloway. It fell into disuse as a thoroughfare by the late 18th/early 19th century. The Bridgnorth to Shrewsbury Road, which crosses Wenlock Edge at Harley Hill, is known to have been in existence in AD1102. In 1675 Harley Bank was known as Wenlock Pitch. The Wenlock Edge road remains a strategic link between south Shropshire and the Severn valley to this day.

Big houses, lordly estates

A particularly significant feature of the historic landscape is the string of estates with their attendant large houses situated along the eastern flank of Wenlock Edge. Following the Dissolution of Wenlock Priory by Henry VIII in 1540, former monastic lands were sold to wealthy individuals who built fine houses set in designed landscapes. Thus Wilderhope, Shipton, Larden and Lutwyche Halls and their attendant lands, became an established part of the local landscape. There was a period of great rebuilding of timber framed buildings in stone in the 17th century; a fashion that was mirrored in many other shire counties at the time. This signifies a golden period of prosperity in the English countryside which was largely derived from fortunes gained from sheep farming.

Wilderhope Manor

The coming of the railway

Agriculture apart, it is the mineral resource of Wenlock Edge that has resulted in major landscape change, not least in the number of large quarries that have eaten into the northern half of the Edge.

The limestone industry was at its height in the mid 19th century and was the principal justification for the construction, in the mid 19th century, of a railway line by the Great Western Railway between Marsh Farm Junction on the Hereford-Shrewsbury railway and Buildwas Junction on the Severn Valley line. The first

Above: **An old railway bridge near Easthope**
Below: **A straight, open section of old railway trackbed below Easthope Wood**
Right: **Remnants of old railway trackbed near Presthope tunnel entrance**

section, from Much Wenlock to Presthope, opened on 5th December 1864, linking the limestone quarries on Wenlock Edge with the Coalbrookdale iron works and beyond. Three years later, the link between Presthope and Marsh Farm Junction was completed. It opened to passenger traffic on 16th December 1867. For the next 80 years, the railway became a firmly established part of the local economy, employing numerous local people and providing links with the burgeoning industrial landscapes of the West Midlands and South Wales. Whilst the line was initially conceived for the carriage of freight and livestock, it rose to prominence as a passenger-carrying railway served by stations at Harton Road, Rushbury, Longville, Easthope Halt, Presthope, Westwood Halt, Much Wenlock and Farley Halt.

The demise of the railway

The end of World War II ushered in the end of the line for, in the light of greatly diminished numbers of passengers, the decision was taken in 1951 to close the line to passenger traffic and in consequence, all the stations and between Much Wenlock and Craven Arms. The last passenger train left Craven Arms for Wellington on 29th December 1951. Following closure to passenger traffic, it was retained for freight between Longville and Much Wenlock, principally for the conveyance of animal feed. Some limestone traffic was still operating from Westwood Sidings at this time. Interestingly, a half mile section of track was retained at Marsh Farm Junction to enable the Royal train to be stabled overnight when members of the Royal family were visiting Central Wales and the Borders. The station at Much Wenlock finally closed to passenger traffic on 21st July 1962 and in 1963, freight working finished between Longville and Much Wenlock. In the following year freight working north of Much Wenlock was withdrawn.

After closure, most of the infrastructure was removed, apart from some of the station buildings which were sold off for conversion as houses. Over time the line began to disappear beneath trees and scrub vegetation. Today the only visible evidence of the railway remains in cuttings, embankments, former station buildings and road bridges. The tunnel through the Edge, just south of Presthope station, is now occupied by bats as opposed to trains hauled by steam locomotives.

The First Edition Ordnance Survey maps published in the late 19th century, when the line was at its height of operation, reveal the extent of sidings, inclines and other features associated with the railway and the limestone industry. It was very extensive and would have been extremely busy at the height of its operating years.

The coming of the railway was perhaps the most momentous event that influenced the landscape of Wenlock Edge. Its closure, after a relatively short working life, saw the Edge revert to the peaceful place it had been in former times, with its woodland filled with birdsong as opposed to the noise and smoke of a working steam railway.

Wenlock Edge today

Nowadays Wenlock Edge is a place of peace and beauty, revered for its historic heritage, magnificent views, flora and fauna. This is in stark contrast to how it was not so very long ago, when the quarries were at their busiest and the woods were full of people cutting the coppice and making charcoal. Although its historical past is now silent and largely hidden beneath the trees, it is there for those who are prepared to look for it. An old map and a keen pair of eyes can make any walk through this woody wonderland a rewarding experience; it is just possible that previously unrecorded archaeological features may be discovered by people enjoying a country walk. The Edge is a subtle blend of the historic past with nature. The archaeology is the 'icing' on a cake made up of many layers.

WHERE TO SEE HISTORIC LANDSCAPE FEATURES

Blakeway Coppice – woodbanks
Holly Coppy, Easthope Wood – hollow ways and woodbanks
Near Lutwyche Hall – charcoal hearth and woodbanks and hollow ways
Longville – charcoal hearths, hollow ways and woodbanks
Wilderhope – field boundaries
Wilderhope Coppice and Stanway Coppice – good hollow way network
Stanway Coppice – hollow way
Presthope, Longville – railway relics

Limestone Industry

by Glyn Williams

Limestone was first obtained from Wenlock Edge during the Roman period for the construction of villa buildings at Yarchester and at Much Wenlock itself. During period 1190 – 1240, when much of the present Priory was built, quarrying began in earnest. Around 1400 quantities of 'building lyme' were supplied to Caus Castle and in 1594 sixteen loads of stone were sent to repair Shrewsbury School. However it was not until the early eighteenth century that we see detailed evidence of commercial exploitation and from the late eighteenth that the industry assumes true importance

The Living Edge – A wanderer's guide to Wenlock Edge · National Trust

In the years 1789–90 there were 13 lime burners on the Wynnstay Estate (the present Gaskell Estate), who collectively produced 3,503 wagon loads of lime and limestone. It was however, only within the last 200 years or so that observers noted the growing importance of the Wenlock limestone industry.

1862 saw Wenlock linked by rail to the East Shropshire Coalfield and the Black Country, but only by the Severn valley route via Shrewsbury or Kiddiminster, a track having been laid from Buildwas. This was later extended, first to Presthope in 1864 and later to Marshbrook Junction in 1867, thus making limestone south of the town more readily accessible. In 1865 John Fowler, Railway Engineer, in his report to the Directors of the Wenlock Railway Company, wrote '...*during the past six months the portion of this line (Wenlock to Presthope) has been opened for mineral traffic... and a large traffic in limestone has been carried which is steadily increasing*'.

Apart from a spike in demand precipitated by the 1914–18 War, the limestone trade declined after the later nineteenth century. The official Wenlock Guide Book of 1933 states '...*this industry (limestone) has experienced lean years, but is rapidly passing into a more prosperous period*'. In fact, this prosperous period did not materialise until the onset of the Second World War, when demand for ground limestone for soil fertilisation regenerated the industry. In the post war years the industry was relatively buoyant.

Centuries of quarrying and lime-burning have had a dramatic impact upon the dip face of Wenlock Edge but have brought prosperity, diversity and character to its people, shaped its traditional buildings and underpinned its employment base. In 1979 approximately 100 people, some 15% of the local workforce were employed, directly or otherwise, in the industry.

In small measure the limestone has been an inspiration for place names, for example Quarry Piece Field, off Blakeway Lane, Kiln Leasow, off Stretton road, Rock Field, above Sytche Coppice and the Rock House Inn and Limeman's Arms, both now defunct. In greater measure perhaps, limestone quarrying had an influence on the coming of the railway to Much Wenlock, with (at that time) all its attendant advantages.

Opposite and top right: **Lea Quarry**
Right: **Railway tunnel at Presthope**

The general background of the industry

In the early days the quarries (often referred to then and until recent times, as the 'Rocks') were small and were worked in a primitive way. Often people combined other occupations such as cow keeping and beer selling, with quarrying and lime burning; even with other sources of income, it appears that these were on a small scale and not very profitable. There are numerous instances down the years of quarriers finding difficulty in making their enterprises pay. Just two examples: Francis Southerne a 'lymemaker' who died in 1730, was heavily in debt and John Bebb was described in the 1831 census as a 'pauper lime burner'. In fact, some of the smaller quarries, where burnt lime was the chief product, were not worked in the winter months. Tools were of the simple type and remained in use until the introduction of mechanical appliances for the extraction, transportation and processing of the stone. Old quarry inventories include rammer bars, heavy hammers, wheelbarrows and stone rakes.

The first procedure in quarrying limestone is the removal of the layer of topsoil from above the rock. This layer of soil is known as 'overburden' or 'bearing'. Originally shovels and wheelbarrows were required to perform this operation, which required the removal of between 20 and 500mm (around 1 to 20 inches) of soil.

Although gunpowder was invented sufficiently early for there to be references to cannon in the stores of the Tower of London in 1388, it wasn't applied to the

Left: **Lea Quarry**
Opposite: **Core Drill**

blasting of rock until early in the seventeenth century (in Saxony in 1627). In this country it does not appear to have been used until a much later date. Before the use of mechanical drilling (to insert the explosive charge) holes in the rock were bored by hand. The drilling of the hole, approximately 35mm (1.5 inches) in diameter, was often carried out by a two man team; one man supported and turned the rammer bar or 'jumper', to which a leather tongue was often attached to avoid jarring, whilst the other wielded a 7 to 11kg (15 to 25lbs) hammer. The rammer bar was around 2m (6 to 7 feet) in length and had two cutting edges at its point which were lubricated by water being poured down the hole. Prior to the Great War, men who were working 'piecework' at this job in the Westwood and Presthope quarries, often brought their drills and rammers down to the blacksmith's shop in St. Mary's Lane to be sharpened. They would then return to their quarries by getting a free ride in the open trucks of the G.W.R. goods train, which travelled each morning to Westwood, Presthope and beyond. It was not uncommon for the quarry 'blower', the quarryman responsible for detonating the explosive charges, to start work as early as 4am to ensure enough loose stone was ready for the start of the day's work.

Before the use of gelignite and other modern explosives, black powder was used for blasting the rock. This was ignited by a naked fuse that had been inserted down each vertically drilled and charged hole. When fuses were not available it was not uncommon to use wheat straw stems joined together and filled with black powder.

Inevitably, with such haphazard use of dangerous explosives, it was not uncommon for accidents to happen. At Bradley Quarry in July 1832 for example, Thomas Trevor was killed in a blasting accident. He was

Above: **Donkey hut/ explosives store at Knowle Quarry**

Below: **Hopper–type trucks**

feeding powder down a borehole whilst his assistant, Joe Hill, was waiting beside him with a lighted piece of paper. A spark from the paper prematurely ignited the powder with the result that Trevor made an instant and non–returnable journey to his maker. Two years later William Carter was blown up whilst blasting rock at an unspecified quarry. He was drunk at the time and a colleague said "...he (Carter) was blown to a great height and landed 20 yards from the blast hole and did not speak again" At the Lilleshall Quarry, H. Lilyman injured his hand when an explosive charge did not go off as quickly as usual and back at Bradley Quarry, around the turn of the century, an unnamed quarry worker injured his arms and eyes in a blasting accident.

On a lighter note, one irate quarryman, not liking the unenviable task of emptying the quarry bucket toilet, decided the most thorough and efficient way was to use a stick of explosive.

Nowadays, limestone is bored with a pneumatic drill and the explosive is detonated electrically by remote control. After blasting operations the quarrymen had to reduce, either at the quarry face or kiln top, the size of some of the limestone by wielding sledgehammers or by using bars and wedges. Most of the men cut their own hazel wood staves for their hammers as evidently this wood is a good absorbent of jarring. Transportation of the limestone from the quarry floor to the kiln top and beyond depended on the site and the date. In the very early days transport would have been

by packhorse, using special horse panniers or horse and cart. The cost of keeping a horse for working in a quarry was 4/8d (24p) per week in 1842. The cost of keeping a donkey may have been cheaper as evidently one was employed at the Knowle Quarry as late as the first quarter of the nineteenth century.

From around the middle of the nineteenth century until after the Second World War, narrow (2 feet) gauge tramways were the chief means of transport; although as early as 1801, a plate way was being used on an inclined plane between the crest and the foot of the scarp slope of Wenlock Edge. The early trucks on the tramways would probably have been small four wheeled vehicles with square or rectangular wooden bodies, but in later years a V–shaped hopper–type, of one to one and half tons capacity, was introduced. The design was for ease of unloading, the body swinging on a frame. These trucks (often called 'tubs' or 'boxes') if they were not hauled by a horse, were either pushed by hand or, in the last few years of their use, pulled along by means of a wire rope attached to a stationary engine, or in the case of Westwood Quarry, hauled by a petrol engine locomotive, the last driver of which was 'Codger' Luscott. This loco was thought to be of German origin and was sold for scrap in 1954. The last tramways were used in the 1950s at Westwood Quarry and at Wenlock (Hayes) Quarry. The system was to transport the raw material from the base of the quarry face to the processing plant by motor truck or dumper, the loading of the dumper being carried out by a mechanical grab or motor shovel.

The allocation of workman's tasks must clearly have varied from quarry to quarry. However, the typical division of labour seems to have been fairly consistent since the early systematic working of quarries until after

The Coalbrookdale Company was paying quarrymen 1/4d (7p) per day in 1776 but by 1830 the going rate appears to have been between 10/- (50p) and 11/- (55p) per week, with somewhat less for the lowest paid workers at the kiln head. This compares with a wage of 3/- (15p) per day at the end of the 19th century, 4.5d to 6d (2p to 3p) per hour in the early 1920s, 9d to 10d (around 4p) per hour in the early 1930's, £3 to £4 per week prior to the onset of World War II, £7 per week in the immediate post war period, 3/- (15p) per hour in the 1950s and something in excess of £30 per week in the 1970s. In the latter three instances the working day varied between eight and ten hours per day and production bonuses were paid.

Above: Mobile crusher/grader
Below: Primary crusher at Lea North Quarry

the Second World War, when the advent of mechanical handling of the limestone revolutionised the industry. A quarry master describing his quarry and lime works in Scotland in 1757 wrote '...*two men for boring and blasting, three for breaking and filling the 'kill', one that draws the lime from the kill, slakes and delivers and one more that has a two horse cart for loading the stone from the quarry to the level at the top of the kill'.*

With this team he considered it a good days work to break ten 'bolls' of stone (about 2.5 tons of lime). Apart from the very small one or two man operated concerns, and the very big enterprises; these arrangements would have been typical in most Wenlock quarries.

Up to 1939, however, men were often employed on a 'piecework' basis, usually being paid by the tub or box of limestone extracted or by the tub of lime taken from

Lime spreader

earned between them in the streets of Shrewsbury on a Saturday afternoon. Because of serious unemployment in the quarries in 1923, the Town Council (to stimulate demand for stone) asked the surveyor to seek a grant from the County Council to repair local roads. Regular employment before the First World War was even more scarce; in 1909 three notable ladies of the town, Lady Gaskell, Mrs. Cooke (wife of Alderman Cooke of the Cooke Clock and Corris House fame) and Mrs. Danks (wife of the National School Headmaster) opened a soup kitchen for the children of the unemployed.

The uses of limestone

The general trend of the industry seems to have been that the quarries around Wenlock produced lime and limestone chiefly for building and agricultural purposes (prior to Darby's iron smelting discovery that created a greater demand for limestone). Although it should not be overlooked that iron smelting furnaces, requiring limestone in their charges existed at Coalbrookdale before Darby's discovery. The furnace charge then was 98lbs (44kg) of limestone to 224lbs (100kg) of ironstone.

Reflecting the demand for limestone for fluxing, thus creating new jobs in the quarries, the parish population rose by 22% in the years 1801–31.

Around the middle of the 19th century there was, to the north of the town and nearer to the ironworks, a general shortage of good limestone for fluxing, but with the building of the railway in 1862–64 the problem was somewhat resolved, as then the limestone southwest of Wenlock became both more accessible and cheaper to transport. But it was still not as cheap as limestone bought by the iron foundries from North Wales. Also in

the kiln. At the beginning of the 1920s quarry workers were being paid 10d (4p) per tub, having first broken by hand the limestone into acceptable sizes, (around 6 inches or 15 cm for burning). The tub was either pushed by hand or hauled by a horse along a tramway to the kiln top or loading wharf, the horse usually being led by the youngest employee, often a youth having recently left school.

When times were hard, through inclement weather or the depressed state of the industry, pieceworkers often supplemented their incomes by working on local farms hoeing, hedge brushing, pulling root crops, harvesting grain, etc. The more innovative sought other methods; in the poor times of the early 1930s four quarriers regularly went Morris dancing. Up to 12/- (60p) could be

the wake of the railway, larger enterprises interested in fluxing stone production became established, in what was hitherto the domain of the local quarrier and lime burner. However, the railway came too late to benefit from the peak years of the iron trade.

From the 1860s onwards demand gradually declined, in part because by that time, Germany and the U.S.A. in particular, had started their own heavy industries, which resulted in a cut back in iron production locally. This caused a decline in fluxing demand, which was reflected in the reports of the Directors of the Much Wenlock and Severn Valley Railway. Firstly in 1863 when they made the observation *'no ironmasters have availed themselves to the Railway Company for the carriage of limestone to their furnaces'*. This was because the spur from Buildwas to Coalbrookdale (which would give direct access, not only to the East Shropshire Coalfield, but also to the main Shrewsbury – Birmingham line) had not been completed. Secondly, in 1867 the Directors reported with regret, *'that owing to the depression in the iron trade gross receipts for haulage are down on the previous year'*. Thirdly in 1870, they stated, 'The diminuation in the traffic still continues and chiefly arises from the falling off in the limestone trade'. To add weight to their concern, the Borough of Wenlock Express of 16th. December 1876 stated that 'Mills and forges are almost destitute of orders and slackness is the rule'.

The demand for agricultural lime was even less brisk. In the 1820s there occurred a general fall in the requirements for lime, due to a combination of over-liming in previous years, over production of cereals and, as it probably concerned Wenlock quarries directly, the adverse effect of the 1822 Turnpike Act. This made lime subject to Turnpike Duty, penalising farmers and producers alike. From the 1830s to the 1870s trade

picked up, albeit modestly, but towards the end of the century a recession was again experienced (aggravated by cheap grain imports from Australia, New Zealand and Canada); this lasted until 1914 and the commencement of the First World War.

At the start of the war farmers were only producing 20% of the nation's wheat requirements and as a whole could only feed the country for 125 days. Demand for home produced food between 1914 and 1918 stimulated the lime trade, but this demand fell away again in the depression years of the twenties and thirties. A further factor that depressed the lime trade in the early part of this century was the mistaken belief that chemical fertilisers made lime unnecessary.

A welcome hiccup occurred in 1927 when the Arlscott Beet Factory was opened. Farmers growing sugar beet needed lime to combat acidity in the soil. In 1939 the agricultural lime trade took a dramatic turn for the better when, with the onset of the Second World War, it became necessary to produce more home grown food.

A subsidy of £2 per acre was introduced to encourage farmers to plough permanent grassland for cereals. From the middle of the war until the mid-sixties (the peak year was 1956) ground limestone for agricultural fertiliser was at a premium. But demand was seasonal, spring and autumn being the peak periods, leaving the quarries virtually idle in the winter months. Burnt lime could not be produced in

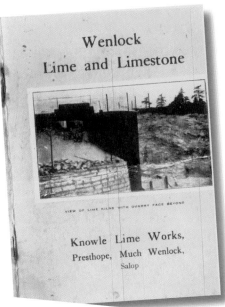

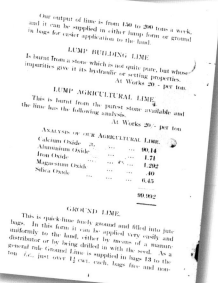

Knowle Lime Works catalogue cover and one of its pages

sufficient quantity and also it became too costly to manufacture. However, after the mid-sixties, due to a general cut back in government subsidies to farmers to purchase lime, (at its height the subsidy was 65%) plus a mild recession in the farming industry, the agricultural lime trade took another downward turn and has remained so.

Nevertheless, with the nearness of the Wenlock limestone quarries to, what was, Dawley New Town and later Telford New Town Development, plus a greater demand generally for road making materials, a dramatic switch was made to the production of aggregates, hardcore and road making stone. This probably saved the Wenlock limestone trade from virtual extinction, as these products were the mainstay of the industry.

Lime in building

Wenlock's knobbly limestone was used for walling only very locally because it was of less economic value than Shropshire's commoner and more workable sandstones. However for mortar, it had an excellent reputation. It was especially the area of the Knowle Quarry around Presthope, where the limestone is crammed with banks of corals, bryozoa and crinoids, that was most favoured for the production of good fat lime putty from quicklime to be used in mortar making. Slaking will have taken place either at the point of production or use. Between 1890 and 1930, Wenlock limestone was used in the manufacture of cement. Burnt and slaked lime was also used in the glass-making and ceramics industries for glazing, as well as in making limewash.

Flare or intermittent kilns

The most common type of limekilns on Wenlock Edge were flare kilns (also known as pot, periodic or field kilns) which were used intermittently. The kilns were loaded, fired, cooled and emptied, and refilled for the next firing. Originating probably in the sixteenth century, they had become common near arable land throughout the eighteenth and nineteenth centuries. Built into slopes and roadside banks, such kilns usually consisted of a brick-lined 'pot' some three metres in diameter at the top, tapering to a narrow neck at the bottom like an inverted cone.

Top: 1950s Quarry face
Middle: Remains of Ballstone Quarry pot kiln (off Blakeway Lane)
Bottom: Kiln in Lilleshall Quarry by the old railway track

At the base of the cone would be a small arch, facing the prevailing wind, to give access to the grate for the draught. Most of these kilns occur singly, but in time more elaborate forms were developed. Some would be buttressed to strengthen their outer walls against internal pressures. A few are doubles, heart shaped in plan, and which generally share a stone or brick draw arch big enough for the lime-worker to enter.

The initial charge of limestone would be formed into a dome resting on a ledge around the side of the grate at the pot base. Smaller pieces of limestone were then loaded on top to fill the kiln, which was left open at the top. A fire was lit under the dome, usually using timber or underwood to deliver modest heat to dry and set the charge. This would be followed by fierce heat using charcoal, coal or latterly coke.

A huge number of oaks were consumed in the smaller intermittent kilns before the introduction of coal. Approximately two cubic metres of oak (1500kg) or over three cubic meters (2000kg) of fir were required to produce a tonne of lime in a simple flare or intermittent kiln.

Once the required temperature had been reached, indicated by a clear red flame at the top, the stoke-hole was partly blocked with earth and stones for 24 to 36 hours to allow the kiln to cook gradually so as to avoid unnecessary damage to its structure, such as might be brought about by a sudden fall in temperature. Once cool, the quick-lime was drawn or dug out using long-handled rakes or shovels. The complete operation probably took about four days. Kilns required continual repair and new kilns were built re-using material from old kilns

Continuous firing kilns

After about 1750 larger kilns capable of working continuously were developed to cater for an increasing demand for burnt lime. Unlike flare kilns, these so-called perpetual or running kilns were kept going with a constant supply of raw material and by regular drawing of the quicklime (calcium oxide).

Typically, these consisted of groups, or banks, of fire-brick lined, conical or necked cylindrical pots designed to withstand continuous firing and to maintain a steady temperature over long periods. Limestone was loaded into the active kiln in layers alternating with coal, charcoal or coke, at a ratio of three to five parts limestone to one of fuel. Movable iron bars at the base of the pot provided support for the charge and could be adjusted for drawing off the lime. Arched openings below the base of each pot, high enough for a man to stand, allowed access to the draw-holes. Such kiln banks were usually built into the hillside, having a front retaining wall or casing strongly constructed of the local stone. The bank of kilns at Knowle is a good example of the type.

Once ignited, fire would spread progressively from its seat throughout the kiln. As quicklime was drawn off, fresh layers of limestone and coal were loaded into the top. Continuous kilns could produce between ten and fifteen tons of lime a day, enough to service some four acres used as a soil conditioner.

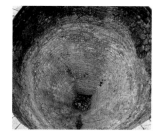

Top: **Knowle Kiln fired in 2005**

Middle: **Looking down into Knowle Quarry Kiln**

Bottom: **Burnt limestone at the base of kiln adit of Knowle Quarry kiln 2005**

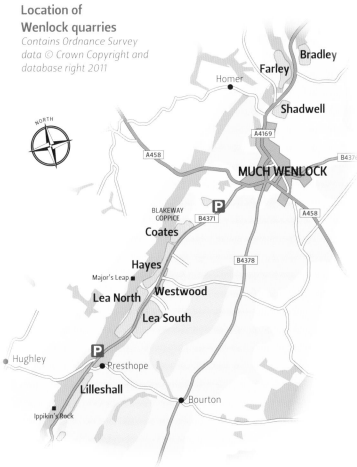

Location of
Wenlock quarries
*Contains Ordnance Survey
data © Crown Copyright and
database right 2011*

Left: Continuous fired steel kiln at Plough Quarry
(Presthope) c1925

Opposite: Lea North Quarry

Knowle Cottage

National Trust and Wenlock Quarries

By Jeremy Milln

Around 1875, with the benefit of the 1867 Much Wenlock – Craven Arms railway line, the Haywoods built a large, continuous burning type lime kiln bank, with four separate pots (SO 58669770) to the north-east of Knowle Cottage. This kiln bank could supply burnt and slaked lime for the iron industries at Coalbrookdale and the Black Country via Presthope station opposite. A narrow gauge two foot tramway was laid from the quarry face to the top of the lime kilns, the wagons being probably pulled by ponies. Associated with the works are the cottage and donkey shed and explosives store (repaired by the Trust in 1993), and the remains of the tramline, well and office. Further archaeological work is required to identify other structures, including that marked on the 1902. 1:2500 Ordnance Survey map adjacent to the Stretton-Wenlock road as 'Old Limekiln.'

The Haywood family were to retain Knowle up until the 1890s with Letitia Haywood noted as a limeburner in 1870, and Elizabeth, George and Henry Haywood as limeburners in 1891.

Henshaw not only burnt limestone at Knowle, but also horse flesh. Carcasses from the knackers' yard in Longville were brought by rail to Presthope stations and from there to Knowle, where he utilised one of the lime kilns to produce bone dust for the china and pottery industry, in which it was used to whiten the clay. Poor business seems to have been the reason behind this diversification.

Victor Deacon came to live at the cottage about 20 years later, remaining until his death in 1991; he had determined that it should not be swallowed by an enormous road-stone quarry just yards from his boundary. Thanks to a legacy, the property at Knowle was acquired by the Trust together with a modest croft, all of its kilns and a cottage. It had always been the intention that the Trust, once the costs could be met, would restore at least one of the pots of the Haywood's kiln to workable order and conserve the remainder. In 1993 a volunteer work party cleared the site of damaging vegetation including young trees; then in 1999 the work to the fabric was undertaken by Treasure & Son of Ludlow. A circular walk was devised with the help of volunteers to give access to sites of interest. In 1999 the kilns were restored and fired up to produce lime mortar for restoration of local buildings.

Knowle limekilns before restoration

Wheelchair paths constructed by NT volunteers at Presthope car park

Beginning the restoration of Knowle limekilns

Restoration in progress

Knowle limekilns now

SOURCE: From original text by Glyn Williams *'The Wenlock Limestone Industry'* published thesis 1990 with edits and alterations by Pete and Kate Johnson and some inserts from the paper *'The Wenlock Edge Limestone Industry'* by Jeremy Milln, NT Archaeologist.

Landscape & Seasons:
Spring

When spring ignites the green fuse which burns through woods and hedges along the Edge, it sparks the moments which define the season. In recent years the weather has blown hot and cold, messing about with the onset of spring. Because of this, there is hardly a season with a beginning and an end any more; it's a steady bursting of moments spluttering from the space we once called winter.

It can be the moment when the first daffodil flowers, but that's been known at Christmas; the moment the first bumblebee blunders through sunshine; or the moment the first frogspawn appears in the pond at half an hour past dawn on a February morning. The most decisive moments are when blackbirds begin singing and Shropshire damsons are caught by the white pulse and burst into snow. When this happens, even if winter is reluctant to leave and snow swirls in the desperate last gasps of Arctic winds, it will founder, to be wrecked against the inevitable reefs of spring.

On a sunny path along the boundary between pasture and woods, peacock and small tortoiseshell butterflies flicker down their own proprietary lines just as they did at the end of last year. Could these individuals be the same ones I saw just as the first frosts came? Have these butterflies turned a seasonal page by surviving winter to carry on where they left off?

When the temperature rises, spring can go hell-for-leather and yet a haze across woods and fields can lock in a weirdness here. The sun quickens the pulse of spring; there is something desperate about its speed as it careers around the seasonal bend. Towards what? For the moment though, the stored energy in earth and tree is enough to ignite the fireworks of renewal. It seems impossible not to get in the way of it. To step outside is to collide with bee lines, hover-fly investigations, aerial dancing troops of midges, zapping butterflies and birds foraging for nesting materials.

Birds are engrossed in what Ted Hughes described in his poem *'Spring Nature Notes'* as "zipping and unzipping / Changing their minds, in soft excitements". With all springs perhaps, there is a recklessness in the air, a contagious disregard for propriety and prudence which, sweeping

away the dour greys, feels exhilarating. And we need that iconoclastic creativity around us now. The predictions for the impacts of human-induced climate change are left hanging and few watching the frantic exuberance of spring life from birds to blossom will want to think about the wave of extinctions slowly gathering.

On Windmill Hill there are splashes of pink star flowers in the grass. They only occur in places where rabbits have nibbled the sward down to the quick and dug shallow divots. This plant is storksbill and when the pink flowers finish, the long beak-like carpels twist in clusters all facing the same direction. It's a fascinating plant with pinnate leaves, kept short by rabbit grazing. It's an annual and is usually found along coasts, sea cliffs and dunes. These dry exposed conditions are what the rabbits create on the banks.

Walking across fields at the foot of the Edge, I listen out for the cuckoo. The noise of birds from the woods is wild. I'm listening to one small stretch of woodland, perhaps half a mile long, only a tiny section of a continuous ribbon of trees which stretches from the Severn Gorge down to Craven Arms, 20 miles away. The breeze has cleared the air of the aural dust which glues to hot dry days and is sweeping through the woods, gathering the songs of birds. The birds, ecstatic now with their own songs and buoyed by the collective power of all the other singers around them, are delirious. From where I stand, the woods above me are like speakers from which comes a wild, anarchic music, amplified by the breeze flowing into and along the Edge. Inside the woods, the crackling energy which gives voice to birdsong, is also surging through the vegetation. Depending on the nature of the slope, the ground has drifts of bluebells, now in flower with their narcotic scent swirls under leafing trees, or massed, near-vertical lawns of Wild garlic on the cusp of bursting into a constellation of white stars. In amongst all this is a plant called toothwort, a strange pigment-less parasite whose leafless, ghostly flowers emerged from the earth bringing a note of mysterious stillness.

When it's raining hard, there can be such a greyness of the sky and a soupy thickness of the verdure, that everything is seen through a fragment of a broken lens which only refracts green light; the focus draws back from the small, intimate, jewel-like things to a murky middle-distance. The Wrekin, to the north, is invisible. The hills of South Shropshire and the Marches have vanished, as have the Clee hills also. Beyond a few miles there is a heavy mist as impenetrable as steamed-up windows. Beyond this could be a vast surrounding fen of rainwater. There is certainly one coming in the sky. The rain gathers slowly from an insistent drizzle; even when it starts hammering down a lone Blackbird refuses to stop singing. It dares the rain, it dares everything and it will not finish with spring yet.

When the sky's sponge is finally wrung dry, a song thrush begins singing from the top of an old damson tree. The weather changes again. Blackthorn is bursting under beams of sunlight plunging from a sky still brimming with energy. Buzzards mew and a woodpecker bounces through clear air. A skylark sparks up above the fields. In the woods, violets flower: the pale lilac of early dog violet, the darker common dog violet and the white of sweet violet. These small, fragile looking flowers pack a big emotional punch at this time of year. Often overlooked in favour of showier blooms and blossoms, the violets speak of an ephemeral world and a history which has slipped into obscurity. No longer popular and their romantic folklore forgotten, these small enigmatic flowers scatter their blue notes through the darker, sodden corners of the landscape, too subtle for joy, too bright for melancholy, too fleeting for worldliness.

As if making up for lost time, spring crashes through the gears, accelerating along hedges greening hawthorn buds, flashing over woodland floors sparking white flowers of wood anemone and wood sorrel, flying across the sky to open new ways into this landscape. Long rags of grey cloud drag showers over the hills and when they fall, the rain holds the sting of hail; white percussive buds of ice. The chiffchaff's return is perhaps the most convincing signal. This small anonymous bird holds spring's adventure for us all to share.

A gang of gulls following the Edge north keep low, out of the wind; a raven carries a white egg. A yellowhammer is perched in a hedge; his colours the browns and duns of thorn and hazel in the hedgerow and the bright yellow of the oilseed rape now flowering in the field he looks across. These birds vanish into mist which looks and feels autumnal. But the sounds hidden in the mist can only speak of spring. The calls and songs are an aural equivalent of violets and primroses. But it is the skylarks pouring their songs into the murky sky, with the same inevitability as the stream flowing downhill towards the river, which set the wild, unstoppable pitch of the season, keeping blind faith whatever the weather.

Rooks and rabbits, buzzards and bees; they are all playing with the elements, testing its limits, seizing their moments. Between showers, the birds fling their hail of songs and calls into the air. Bumblebees draw long ribboning lines of ultraviolet through plants. A green fire rages, uncheckable now. The sights and sounds of spring are building with intensity and from the immensity of the sky to the tiniest leaf bud; there is no stillness in the world.

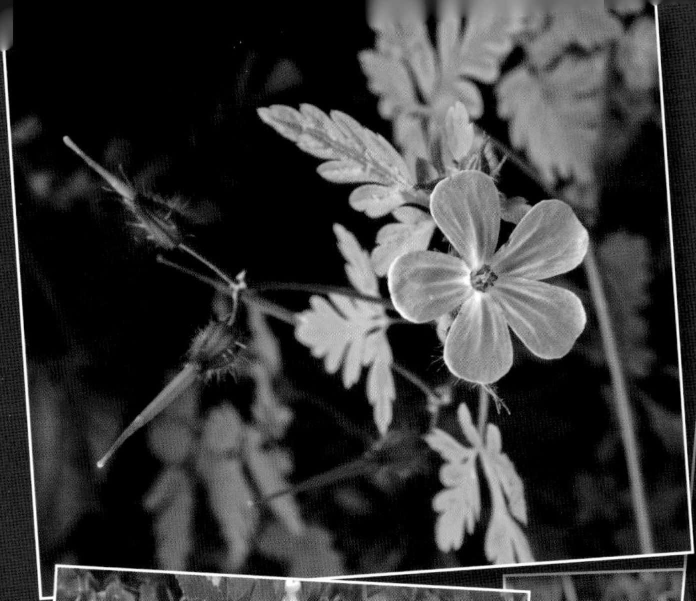

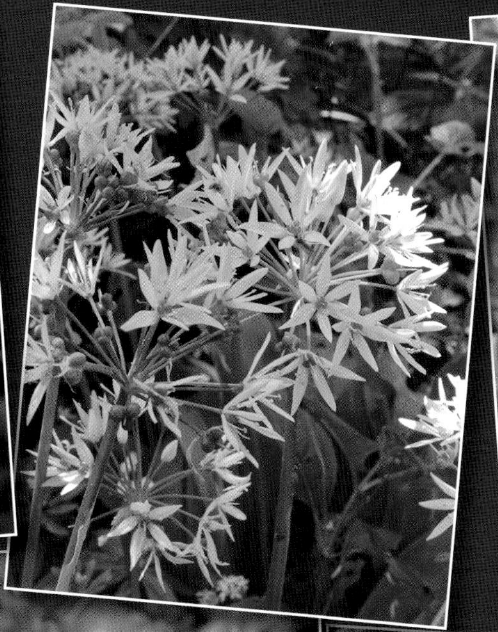

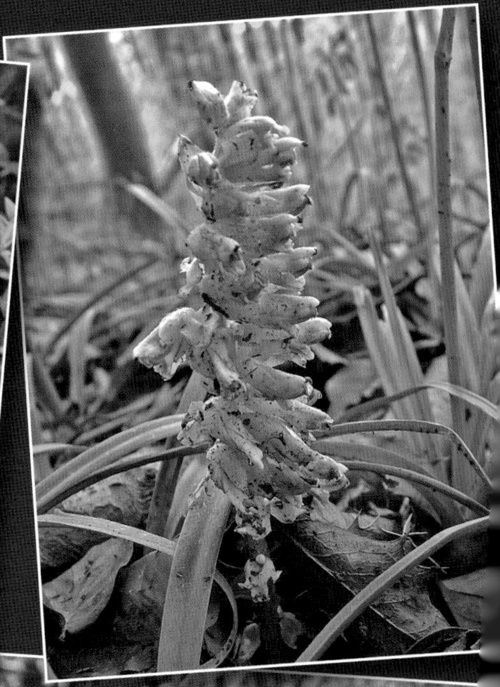

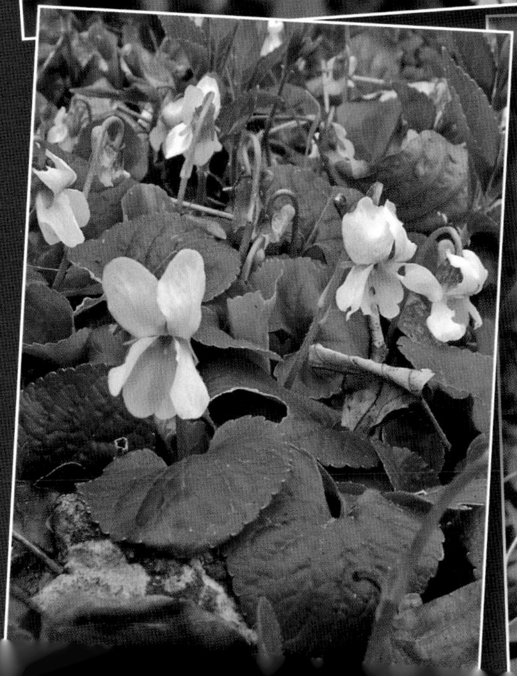

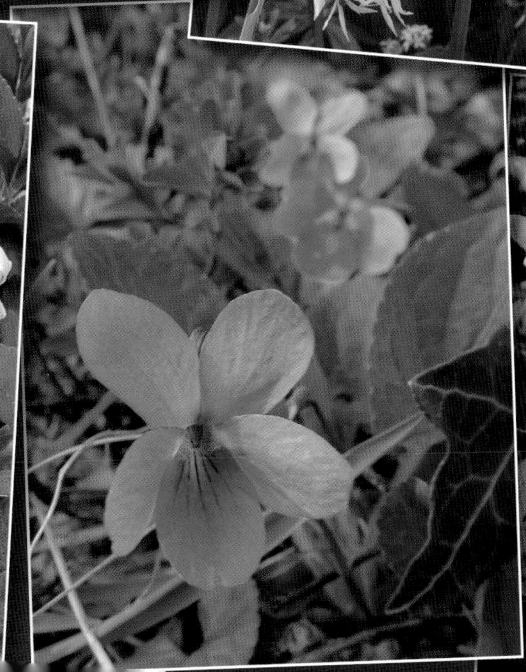

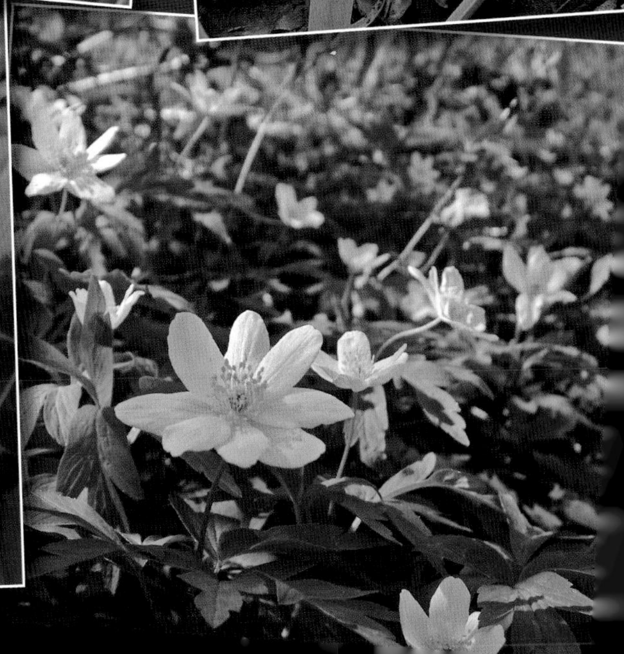

In the old quarry woods, where trees have re-colonised spoil mounds whose shapes echo the clouds above, I listen to the birds. I try not to attach names to sounds. Even though this is a chiffchaff and a nuthatch, I listen to the community of birdsong becoming the texture of the air. The ground is green with new grass blades, tongues of wild garlic and whorls of dog's mercury. Hawthorn, opening in tufts, has a tangy aftertaste. Spindle is almost full out. Hazel is still cautious. A sudden flash of pink reveals flowering currant shrubs, relics of a long-abandoned garden. In an open patch, sunlight catches the tiny opalescent wings of dancing gnats. Between the leaves, between the trees, between the showers, there is no time for stillness, only a frenetic kind of divination where everything seeks a future but nothing wants an answer.

The thunder wakes me into a storm charging through morning. Even when the downpour stops, the air is still ringing wet and fizzing with the static of growth. The fiddleheads of ferns are unwinding and the old green tune they play is as fresh and quick as ever. The leaves of beech, hazel and others that have been shy for weeks are opening wide. All the wild cherry trees are snowy with blossom. Over the woods, there's a silvery-grey sheen as oak buds swell from their dark capsules. The hedgebanks flower white with stichwort, hedge mustard and white deadnettle; there are brimstone-yellow clumps of cowslip everywhere. As the sunshine brightens, the first holly blue butterflies jiggle across the vegetation like dots of cobalt light. Small tortoiseshell and white butterflies join the bumblebees through the spaces full of flower.

The following morning there is another kind of thunder which wakes me; it's the dawn chorus. The birds seem to find their collective mind even though they are of many species and have many songs. From the fluid stream of willow warblers to the clockwork hiccup of pheasants, the birds find their voices at dawn. A chorus is a coordinated response to the episodes of others, a single simultaneous utterance or the bit of the song we all join in on. But this is a phenomenon with quite different dimensions of time and space, which spans the divisions between species and individuals and affects all who hear it. It is the sound of spring, the rushing, roaring, recklessness of growth and rejuvenation. And as if to personify that explosive spirit, the swifts have returned, this changes everything: the weather, the mood and the pace of spring. Through slashing lines and screaming curves, swifts rip up a blue sky above the church fetes and village fairs. These country festivals mark the turning season and have their origins in ancient rituals. But whatever those were, I'm sure the reality is that people still get together to celebrate community and the reckless exuberance of May.

The lanes are white with a bow-wave of cow-parsley and the air is dripping with the sexy musk of May. I walk into the woods along an old path used by quarry workers a hundred years ago. There are blackcaps in the hawthorn and in a crabapple tree a chiffchaff sings; *chiff...chaff...chiff...chaff*, a two-beat song, clear and strong as the left-right of quarry workers' nailed boots on stones. Then the chiffchaff riffs on his metronome, slipping notes and compacting phrases to make the two-step skip, to break the line. Now it's a dance, now it's the sound of ghosts in their boots, dancing in the May woods.

What did these songs mean to the people who worked in the quarries, fields and woods centuries ago? Where did they think the summer migrant birds came from? Such mysteries were as much part of the texture of daily life as its meaning. Are they now? Perhaps. Whatever we learn about the biology of migration it doesn't entirely capture how we feel about it. Our connection with Nature is through the particular; this bird in the here and now. Once we were tied to the land and few of us wandered far. Then the wild ungovernable things which come and go with the seasons were our bridge to the world beyond us, even if that world was a dark mystery. Now we are connecting with people and events around the world in an instant; our culture yearns for a continuity of place and the seasonal signals that wild lives bring. When I get to the far side of the wood, there's a stile which overlooks the long wooded scarp of the Edge, and the plain which stretches westwards to the hills of the Welsh Marches. At dawn it's a thunderous swarm of song. At dusk it's the sound of falling shards of light. To listen is to join it. I feel ghosts dancing in my boots too.

Plants and Vegetation

by Sarah Whild

For any casual observer, dog-walker, visiting naturalist or just the passing motorist on the A49, the dominant visual impact of Wenlock Edge is created by the vegetation. The woodland defines and outlines the geology and land-use of Wenlock Edge, clinging to the escarpment face and remaining on the steepest slopes where agricultural improvement has not been possible.

Above: Dog's Mercury
Right: Herb Paris

Opposite page: Hoary
Plantain

Introduction

Much of the habitat is what is termed 'ancient woodland'; areas of land that have not been ploughed or undergone radical changes in use since the 1600s, when reliable maps were first produced. Other areas of woodland have been felled and replanted with conifers for commercial forestry or have regenerated naturally. The ancient woodland areas are those that provide the breathtaking displays of wild flowers in the spring, the species composition varying with subtle changes in geology and soil. Between the blocks of woodland are pockets of grassland, some of which are quite extensive. The grassland is mostly unimproved agriculturally and has a resulting species-rich sward of grasses, sedges and other herbs.

So, is Wenlock Edge of any great significance for its vegetation apart from producing a prominent landmark in Shropshire? It is notified as a Site of Special Scientific Interest (SSSI) not only for its geology but for its stands of Ash *Fraxinus excelsior*, Wych Elm *Ulmus glabra* and Sessile Oak *Quercus petraea*. These form a distinct community which plant ecologists classify under a system called the National Vegetation Classification. Most of the woodland on the Edge is Ash–Field Maple wood with a Dog's Mercury ground flora; although these are three unremarkable species in themselves, this community (labelled W8 by plant ecologists), is the one most closely associated with lowland species-rich woodlands on calcareous soils (which, in the case of Wenlock Edge are derived from the underlying Silurian Limestone). Such a woodland community often has an abundance of flowering plants in the ground layer producing colourful spring assemblages. This is not a rare woodland type in Shropshire but the stands on Wenlock Edge provide some of the most extensive areas in the county. On the soils towards the bottom of the slopes, Wild Garlic *Allium ursinum* produces a carpet of starry white flowers dominating entire areas of the ground flora in the Spring. Where the soils are leached by rain and weathering on drier slopes, there is a subtle change in the vegetation with Pedunculate Oak *Quercus robur* becoming more dominant. The ground flora shifts from the pungent displays of Wild Garlic to a virtual monoculture of Bluebell *Hyacinthoides non-scripta*, interrupted only by occasional clumps of Broad Buckler-Fern *Dryopteris dilatata* or Male Fern *D. filix-mas*. Occasional pockets of soil with an even more acidic reaction produce variants of the Ash-Field Maple woodland, more akin to upland variants found on Carboniferous Limestone in the Derbyshire Dales, with lush stands of Lady Fern *Athyrium filix-femina*.

Compared to other counties with overlying chalk, Shropshire does not have many great stands of calcareous grassland overlying hard limestone. However, the remnants it does have are particularly interesting to compare and contrast. The Carboniferous Limestone of the north-west of the county underlies fragments of limestone grassland that are quite different in character to the grassland found on Wenlock Edge. Woolly Thistle *Cirsium eriophorum* is a stately plant of small meadows along Wenlock Edge but is virtually absent from corresponding grassland in the north-west of Shropshire, together with Greater Knapweed *Centaurea scabiosa* and Hoary Plantain *Plantago media*. Conversely, Common Rockrose *Helianthemum nummularium* is frequent on the Carboniferous Limestone grassland but absent from the Wenlock Edge

Left: **Male Fern**
Bottom left: **Woolly Thistle**
Below: **Wild Garlic**
Bottom: **Bluebells**
Right: **Broad Buckler-Fern**
Bottom right: **Greater Knapweed**

limestone grasslands. Why are there such differences? There may be minute chemical differences in the soil chemistry or differences in drainage, slope, aspect or management but there are many plant species that are common to all limestone grassland in the county.

Where the limestone has been quarried away, bare rock and thin weathered soils support an almost ephemeral flora that cannot withstand competition from taller grasses and other herbs. Basil Thyme *Clinopodium acinos* and Long-Stalked Cranesbill *Geranium columbinum* form delicate patchworks on the bare ground, together with Small-Flowered Buttercup *Ranunculus parviflorus* and Fairy Flax *Linum catharticum*. On more natural limestone exposures, spring ephemeral species such as Rue-leaved Saxifrage *Saxifraga tridactylites* and Spring Whitlow Grass *Erophila verna* provide a humble early show of small white flowers.

Plant records and the early botanists who recorded there

The earliest plant records for Wenlock Edge were made by the Reverend Edward Williams, who recorded Autumn Gentian *Gentianella amarella* and Flat Sedge *Blysmus compressus* in 1800. Autumn Gentian is still seen in some of the limestone meadows but Flat Sedge has been extinct in the county for many years, not having been recorded since 1886. As a species of calcareous fens and flushes, it was present below Wenlock Edge escarpment but this habitat must have disappeared over a century ago. In 1805 Arthur Aikin recorded Kidney Vetch *Anthyllis vulneraria*, a species typical of calcareous grassland and an important food plant for the Small Blue Butterfly *Cupido minimus*. Yellow-Wort *Blackstonia perfoliata* was also recorded in 1805 by Dr. J. Evans. This member

of the Gentian family is still abundant on the Edge in dry calcareous grassland and is very distinctive, with wide yellow flowers and blue-grey foliage, the leaves of which wrap around the main stem (perfoliate), hence the specific epithet *perfoliata*.

Perhaps the best known name in early plant recording is that of William Penny Brookes, who is often credited with being the founder of the modern Olympic movement. He lived from 1809 to 1895 and worked for most of his career as a doctor in Much Wenlock. He also set up the Much Wenlock School and was a Justice of the Peace. His energies also went into botanical collecting, amassing quite a substantial herbarium which is now in the Much Wenlock museum. Perhaps the most frustrating part of his collection was the lack of detail on the sheets, which means that it is often hard to discern exact locations or dates from many of the specimens. Species that he did make detailed records for on Wenlock Edge include Common Gromwell *Lithospermum officinale*, Long-Stalked Cranesbill *Geranium columbinum*, White Hore-Hound *Marrubium vulgare*, Guelder Rose *Viburnum opulus* and Herb Paris *Paris quadrifolia*. Most of these records are assigned to either 1841 (the date of publication of Leighton's *Flora of Shropshire*) or his date of death in 1895. William Penny Brookes also recorded Field Gentian *Gentianella campestris* (now extinct in Shropshire) at the top of Harley Bank in 1832 and this is the earliest botanical record available from his collection.

William Allport Leighton's 'Flora of Shropshire', published in 1841 gives numerous records for Wenlock Edge; Frog Orchid *Coeloglossum viride* and Lesser Butterfly Orchid *Platanthera bifolia* were both recorded several times in the nineteenth century but both of these species seem to have disappeared from the Edge.

Yellow-Wort

Bryophytes (mosses and liverworts), were first recorded (somewhat half-heartedly) by the Reverend Painter in 1899, who recorded five rather common mosses. In 1913 J.B. Duncan tackled them more systematically and managed to list eighteen species. This was not a site that attracted many of the older cryptogamic (bryophyte and fern) botanists. True site lists that give a proper reflection of the bryophyte diversity of Wenlock Edge were not attempted until the 1970s, when extensive lists by Martin Corely and Martha Newton were compiled. For any visitor to Wenlock Edge, the bryophytes are in places visually significant; on the rock exposures and thin soils overlying the limestone, *Ctenidium molluscum* hugs the substrate closely and in the more open woodlands, *Rhytidiadelphus triquetrus* provides a lush springy layer below the flowering plants and ferns.

Tree species on Wenlock Edge

There are no particularly rare trees on the Edge but perhaps the most notable is the Large-leaved Lime *Tilia platyphyllos* which is a nationally scarce ancient woodland indicator, occurring in fewer than 101 ten-kilometre squares in Britain. Small-leaved Lime *Tilia cordata* is also frequent on the wooded slopes and rides and the two hybridise in Farley Dingle to produce Common Lime *Tilia x europaea*. Although limes tend to be readily identified by their heart-shaped leaves and distinctive fruits, identification of species is often difficult even for experienced botanists due to the prevalence of the hybrid.

Arguably the most interesting species to botanists and ecologists is Wild Service *Sorbus torminalis*, which is related to the Rowan or Mountain Ash. Like the Large-leaved Lime, it is an ancient woodland indicator and

Top: Ctenidium molluscum
Above: **Wild Service**
Opposite: **Broad-leaved Helleborine**

is particularly poor at colonizing new sites due to virtually no seeds from its fruit germinating. It is however, particularly successful at suckering to produce small stands of trees which are all clones of the parent plant. Its older common name is 'Chequer Tree' – before hops were widely used to flavour beer, the fruits of Wild Service were used to give a bitter flavour. As landlords of inns would brew their own ale, a Chequer Tree was often planted in the garden, resulting in the frequent pub or inn name of the Chequers or Chequer Tree.

Rarities, parasites and curious clovers

There are very few rare plant species on Wenlock Edge; Dune Helleborine *Epipactis dunensis*, a nationally rare species (recorded in fewer than 16 ten-kilometre squares in Britain) is arguably the rarest, recorded just once and not since 1978 when it was seen in Blakeway Coppice, together with Narrow-Lipped Helleborine *Epipactis leptochila* and Violet Helleborine *E. purpurata*. Violet Helleborine and Broad-leaved Helleborine *E. helleborine* can still be found in many parts of the woodland.

The helleborines usually flower in July after the spring species have disappeared and provide a fruitful quest for the botanist in later summer. Violet Helleborine is a particularly interesting species, being more or less on the northern edge of its range in Shropshire. It is well adapted to deep woodland with an almost closed canopy, as it produces very little chlorophyll (the green pigment in most flowering plants that allows them to manufacture complex sugars from the sun's energy). Sometimes a form can be found that is entirely purple (leaves as well as flowers) with no chlorophyll. There is speculation as to how it can derive its complex sugars; is it being parasitic or saprophytic?

There are several flowering plants on Wenlock Edge that exhibit more unusual life strategies; Yellow Birds-nest *Monotropa hypopitys* is a strange saprophytic plant that, as the name suggests, is a pale yellow colour throughout, again with no chlorophyll as it obtains its complex sugars from decaying vegetation beneath the soil, as does Bird's-nest Orchid *Neottia nidus-avis*. Although these two plants have a nominal similarity, they are completely unrelated but do have very similar life strategies which mean that they are very well adapted to deep shade and have no need of sunlight. The 'bird's-nest' part of the name refers to a root structure resembling a large untidy bird's nest; this provides a very large surface area for maximum absorption of nutrients from decaying vegetation.

Both of these species are sporadic, particularly the Yellow Birdsnest; one parasitic flowering plant that can be abundant in some years is Toothwort *Lathraea squamaria*. It flowers fairly early in the spring and the first signs of it are ghostly white curved shoots that curl out of the ground (giving it its rather more dramatic 'country' name of 'dead mens' fingers'). These 'fingers' straighten out to produce flowering shoots of white stems, having white flowers with pinkish-brown interiors that resemble a rotten tooth (hence its common name). Toothwort parasitises a range of tree and shrub species, with Hazel, Holly and Lime being amongst its favourite victims. Look for it in early May at the base of Hazel coppice stools, particularly where there has been coppicing work the previous year.

Some parasitic flowering plants on the Edge are not so obviously 'odd' at first glance; Toothwort when first encountered is not a typical plant in so many aspects of its appearance. However, the hay meadows and other grassland areas on Wenlock Edge are often dominated by two species which also rely on a parasitic life style. Yellow Rattle *Rhinanthus minor* is a common species of unimproved hay meadows; areas of grassland that have a very specific management regime where the grassland is left uncut until late summer. When the vegetation is cut and the hay is made, livestock are then turned onto the grassland to graze the 'aftermath' growth.

Any plant that survives in such a regime must be tough and this results in a species-rich sward, with a little help from Yellow Rattle. It can still be possible for the competitive grasses such as Cocksfoot *Dactylis glomerata* to begin to dominate a sward if legumes such as Red Clover *Trifolium pratense* are common. All legumes 'fix' nitrogen and enrich the soil and this increase in fertility can lead to an increase in competitive species such as Cocksfoot.

So what of Yellow Rattle? It is an attractive plant with yellow hooded flowers and green leaves but underground it produces special root-like structures called haustoria which tap into the roots of grasses and legumes to steal sugars and other nutrients. Unlike the Bird's-Nests and Toothwort, Yellow Rattle is capable of manufacturing its own complex sugars as it contains chlorophyll but it can also parasitise its neighbours very effectively, ensuring that no single species dominates the hay meadows. You will see Yellow Rattle in many of the meadows along the Jack Mytton Way on the Edge. Also look out for the tiny white Eyebright *Euphrasia nemorosa*, a close relative which also shares its partially parasitic tendencies.

One final curiosity, present in some years in abundance along the Jack Mytton Way pastures above the woodland, is 'phyllodic' White Clover *Trifolium repens*. This is ordinary White Clover which is infected with a virus or mycoplasma which produces a flower head made up of leaves rather than petals. This is not a particularly rare condition but it is notable in this location for its sheer abundance.

Left: **Toothwort**
Middle: **Yellow Rattle**
Right: **Red Clover**

Opposite page:
Top: **Broad-Leaved Helleborine**
Bottom: **Yellow Bird's-Nest**

Changes in the flora and vegetation

There have without doubt been changes to the flora and vegetation of Wenlock Edge, how much has it changed since Edward Williams botanised here over two hundred years ago? He would have been surprised at the number of conifers planted in the plantation areas and he may have remarked on how little use the grassland areas were put to, with no active lime kilns or limestone extraction and relatively little grazing compared to the nineteenth century. There are probably species that we will not see return to the Edge however sympathetically it is managed; Field Gentian has declined

dramatically throughout lowland England as have the Frog- and Lesser Butterfly Orchids.

The vegetation of Wenlock Edge is as much a product of the past use as of the underlying geology, but the botanist of two hundred years time would hopefully see little change – perhaps the conifers will gradually be returned to species-rich broad-leaved woodland and the unimproved grassland extended from the Edge with habitat creation schemes.

FURTHER READING

Lockton, A.J. & Whild, S.J. 2005. **Rare Plants of Shropshire** 3rd Edition. Shrewsbury: Shropshire Botanical Society.
Rose F. & O' Reilly. 2006. **A Wildflower Key**. Warne.

Sinker, C.A., Packham, J.R., Trueman, I.C., Oswald, P.H., Perring, F.H. & Prestwood, W.V. 1985. **Ecological Flora of the Shropshire Region**. Shropshire Trust for Nature Conservation, Shrewsbury.
Further information from:
Botanical Society of the British Isles
Shropshire Botanical Society, Shropshire Wildlife Trust.

WHERE TO SEE...

Herb Paris: Harton Hollow, along the top path in May.

Wild Service: At the top of Blakeway Coppice, best seen from the Jack Mytton Way, June to October.

Woolly Thistle: In the 'donkey fields' along the Jack Mytton Way, off Blakeway Hollow, in July.

Orchids: Main Wenlock Edge car park near Much Wenlock and Blakeway Hollow, May to July.

Barren Strawberry

Lesser Celandine

Greater Butterfly
Orchid

Eyebright

Meadow at Marked Ash

Grassland

by Pete Carty

Tucked away in sometimes hidden corners, the meadows, pastures and patches of grassland along the top of Wenlock Edge are amongst the best for wild flowers in the Midlands. They support a great diversity of exciting and colourful species which are present in spectacular shows. Most of these meadows are designated as 'Sites of Special Scientific Interest' (SSSIs) by the government agency Natural England. SSSIs are the country's important wildlife and geological sites; they include some of our most inspirational and beautiful places.

Top: **Ippikins Meadow**
Above: **In Lilleshall Quarry**

Context and significance

Why are these flower-rich grasslands found along Wenlock Edge? The key answer to that question is the very substance of the Edge itself, limestone. It is the chemical and physical properties of this rock that directly lead to the floristic richness. This is especially so where limestone is at or close to the surface, with only a thin covering of soil. Any soil derived from these rocks has a high pH and is alkaline, described as 'base-rich' referring to the high levels of basic salts present. The most important basic salt is calcium carbonate.

Many of the special plants growing on the Edge are called 'calcicolous', meaning they are 'lime loving' and require high lime levels in order to grow. Most of these would not be found if the soil lacked calcium. Quite a different flora is found on the nearby Long Mynd where soils are acidic and mineral poor.

Naturally, soils on top of the edge would also have low levels of plant nutrients such as nitrates and phosphates; these soils can be described as having low fertility. This in turn favours flowers and reduces the vigour of grasses. In soils where fertility is high, vigorous 'coarse' grasses such as Upright Brome or False Oat Grass flourish. These grasses smother and shade out the shorter, light-loving flowering plants. So, unless the soil is agriculturally improved by the addition of artificial fertilisers containing Nitrates and Phosphates or they are grazed very heavily all year round, the meadows along the edge will produce good shows of flowers.

The limestone is porous and is dissolved by rainwater containing carbon dioxide from the air. This in turn allows water to percolate through the rock leaving well-drained soils on the surface, which is an additional influence on the types of plants able to survive there.

The bare rock surfaces can become quite warm, especially in sheltered niches, thus creating microclimates typical of conditions much further south. In turn this allows species from more southern regions to occur further north (a factor especially important to a number of insects found).

Elsewhere in Shropshire, flower-rich grasslands like those along Wenlock Edge are to be found in the hills around Oswestry, where limestone also appears on the surface and where old quarries and commons have allowed the flora to survive until today. Good examples of these can be found on Llanymynech Rocks and Llynclys Common.

Outside of Shropshire one has to travel to such places as the limestone areas of Northern England such as the Dales, the dune slacks of the North West (where calcium carbonate from seashells creates the right conditions), or the chalk downs of Southern England to find comparable flower spectacles. These grasslands transport us to the wonderful meadows that used to exist widely across England; meadows that were beloved of landscape painters and poets such as John Clare give us a glimpse of the landscape as it was before agricultural intensification.

Meadow and pasture

Throughout the British Isles the term 'meadow', which is derived from the Old English *mædwe* is widely used to mean a hay meadow. This is grassland that is not grazed from spring onwards and is cut annually in late summer; the cut grass is dried and baled for animal feed as hay. The term 'pasture' is used for land which is primarily grazed, which may include grassland ('grass pasture') but also includes non-grassland habitats such as heathland, moorland and wood pasture. 'Grassland' is used to include both meadow and grass pasture. All of these have been created originally by the clearance of the Wildwood and as late as the last tithe map, the present woodland area of Wenlock Edge contained many fields and pastures which, through neglect, have now returned to woodland. The boundary between woodland and pasture has likely ebbed and flowed over recent centuries.

Transition

Left unmanaged, these meadows and pastures would undergo changes in the composition of plant species and the height of the sward. This is known as (ecological)

Footpath near Easthope Mill

Above: **Crested Dog's-tail**
Top right: **In Lilleshall Quarry**
Right: **National Trust Hebridian sheep in Bellstone Quarry**
Far right top: **Stoke's Barn Quarry**
Far right below: **From Ippikin's Rock**

succession. In the meadows on Wenlock Edge this goes as follows; fine thin grasses left uneaten or uncut become matted and over-winter as fegg or straw, this is followed by invasion of taller coarse grasses e.g. Tor Grass, Cocksfoot and False Oat Grass, in turn followed by Brambles, Hawthorn and then Ash and other trees until high, canopy-closed woodland is achieved. Ultimately some 400 years later ancient woodland is established.

This ecological succession can be seen in the older quarries where removal of rock and disturbance to the surface ceased over 80 or more years ago. It is often possible to see all stages of the successional process, from bare rock to early colonisers such as mosses or small annual plants, followed by the development of a thin soil layer, to grassland with tall herbs and through to woodland. Woodland is the climax vegetation over much of the British Isles. The exceptions to this are salt-blasted coastal heath, alpine meadows on cold mountain tops, or flood plains where other environmental factors prevent the growth of forest.

From the point of view of nature conservation, how do we maintain this grassland in a condition where maximum flower richness continues? We want to do this in order to continue to enjoy the pleasure of walking through these sadly rare habitats. Grazing or cutting is required to retain grassland, combined with low fertility management, i.e. no artificial fertilizers. In addition, the avoidance of pesticides or herbicides which would kill the plants themselves is essential; no insecticides should be used which would kill the insects, which are a vital part of the grassland ecosystem.

National Trust use Hebridean sheep which are one of most ideal breeds for the task. They are a hardy old breed which eat brambles, nettles, docks and even young trees up to a diameter of 20cms. They are a browser as well a grazer, i.e. they will nibble trees and foliage and not just expect lush fertile grass. In this way they mimic the old fashioned breeds of sheep that grazed these pastures and meadows and helped to create and maintain them. Modern breeds of sheep prefer modern swards of improved grass where they produce meat for the modern market. Old breeds will not only eat rough vegetation and unwanted invasive species, they also require very minimal winter feed. This reduces the amount of work required to care for them and avoids the problem of winter feed adding nutrients, hence contributing to increased fertility in the meadow and thus favouring grasses not herbs.

Not all meadows are on old Quarries, for instance Ippikins Meadow opposite the Wenlock Edge Inn is an old farmed meadow, albeit on thin soil, on the crest of a scarp

Bee Orchid

Ragged Robin

Early Purple Orchid

Dyers Greenweed

slope. It has been maintained in the past by this traditional low input farming (and hence low output or low yield). It was saved by the Shrewsbury Horticultural Society who donated it to National Trust. It is currently managed as a hay meadow with some aftermath grazing by Hebridean sheep.

Within the woodland at Wenlock Edge, one can find many relict grasslands on the site of disused quarries, where the trees have invaded over recent decades. At Wenlock this is a process which appears to be complete in about 100 years, due to the presence of much surrounding woodland and large seed-banks of tree species. Hawthorn is typically the first shrub to appear, Ash in particular is a prolific coloniser.

Future of grasslands on Wenlock Edge

It is a concern of conservationists that small patches of habitat, isolated from one another, are less able to withstand change than larger more interconnected ones. A current theme in nature conservation is to work to reduce isolation and increase 'connectivity' of habitats where opportunity allows. This action minimises the impact of adverse events that can eliminate rare and vulnerable species from a particular meadow (such as fire or disease), increasing the opportunity of species moving between habitats and allowing re-colonisation.

The new Higher Level Stewardship scheme offered to landowners to pay for positive conservation work will help this. Already there have been considerable improvements in the quality of grasslands around Blakeway Hollow and Stokes Barn as a result of the removal of scrub and small trees. For many years, some very positive conservation work has been carried out by the Millichope estate in the Rushbury area.

The most exciting opportunity for the creation of new habitats is currently presenting itself in the disused quarries. Such areas if managed carefully could develop the most exciting grasslands. A combination of these actions above will be needed to save the meadows and to give them room to adjust in a changing future world.

Climate change will impact on these meadows. Increased droughts will stress them and reduce grass growth but increased rainfall will promote all-year growth of grasses. Management will have to be adjusted to keep conditions optimal for flowers.

Landscape & Seasons:
Summer

I hear the 'prrrup' of wings around my head and stand still. The dragonfly is flying through a column of air and I've just walked in to it. With quick right-angle twists and turns through an apparently random pattern within a tight space, it darts in and out of focus. At frequent intervals it comes to rest on a limestone rock in the sun with its back to the breeze and then settles, angling its horizontal wings downwards like brakes on an aeroplane and folding its legs so its body lies flat against the warming rock.

This is a ruddy darter, so called because of the scarlet stick of its abdomen, no thicker than a fine knitting needle, belonging to a group of dragonflies for which 'darter' is wholly appropriate.

Even at rest, its head remains hyperactive, twisting and turning with a strange, robotic movement so its enormous compound eyes can take in the world around it. What does it see? I imagine images set in the facets of those eyes like pictures on a hundred camera monitor screens, many images being fragments of things which are constantly being constructed and deconstructed as the head shifts and the world changes. But I also imagine images fixed for a moment in those eyes like memories, a compound of pictures received at random which the mind sorts into meaning.

Summer is full of these visual clues to meaning but often broken into shiny fragments and, like a stained glass window, it tells a story through images. A lesser-spotted woodpecker takes up his position at the top of a dead wych-elm. Pied; black and white with scarlet cap, the little woodpecker drills the humid air with sharp, piping calls. In a brown flash, a sparrowhawk strikes through hawthorns, seeming to pass like a ghost through the lattice of branches without touching it. Wheat crackles as it ripens and from the bare soil on the footpath at the edge of the field a waxcap, a little fungus that looks like a yellow-headed match, emerges as a relic of pastures from long-ago.

Between the fields and Edge Wood, butterflies flicker into sudden presence: gatekeeper, holly blue, speckled wood and meadow brown. Some are already battered by the weather but they cluster in every available pool of sunlight, flickering around each other in knots, feeding from the nectar of thistles and burdock which are also full of bees.

A dead baby bird is wearing the jewellery of flies. It's hardly a bird yet, just a thing made of some light and the flesh of grubs and worms the blue tit parents brought to its tiny gape in the honeysuckle nest. Emerald green flies spin around it then fasten onto its body, sucking up the juice of almost being, of becoming. The story of how this nestling came to splat on the path so far from the nest is written in the stain around it, glistening in a warm summer morning. There will be many more dead squabs before the month is out.

Within a stone's throw are hidden nests of blue tit, sparrow, goldfinch, blackbird, robin, wren and blackcap. Each clutch of eggs has hatched and the parent birds are ramming as much food into the chicks as they can find. Away from the shadows there are flowers everywhere and bees pinballing through the spaces between them.

It's quiet weather, warm, thick with haze, like a headache. Now the wild garlic flowers turn to seed and their leaves yellow, the stink is stronger in the woods. This smell lingers in the memory long after the plants have returned to their bulbs in the clay, their work above ground done for another year. The tree canopy above has closed over the stink, sealing in the shadows; the calls of birds ring through the green. Down on the earth, at the roots of sallow, a grass snake searches for an opportunity to slither into. The snake finds a flow across moist earth towards the ditch and all of it is a continuous movement, a divining rod moving to a rhythm which does not trouble the shadows. Only its eye betrays its snakeness, and if there were any pity in it, this world would fall to pieces.

A gang of swifts twenty to thirty-strong tears through the air above the gardens of Much Wenlock. Few other birds dare go near them. They maintain an altitude of about 30 metres or so, sometimes flinging themselves upward, sometimes diving recklessly into gardens, and screaming all the time. In late evening after a hot, bright day which has brought out the insects, the swifts are scooping up gapes-full of aerial plankton. They have new broods of youngsters to work with; teaching them the devilish tricks of swiftness and cementing bonds for future breeding and the migration back to Africa. Their departure is imminent now, in a few weeks they'll be gone. But for now they make the most of the food the warm weather, pushing at the boundaries of danger with all their manic energy.

I can't say I clocked the exact moment, but as dusk fell and a stealthy cloud cover darkens the sky, the swifts quit screaming over the rooftops and disappeared, to whatever part of the sky they spend the night. What is really noticeable is the quiet.

Apart from a few bats and moths nothing stirs in the air. In a little meadow by the side of a stream, the grass has yet to be cut, it's dry and summer-scented. The silence is curious, especially since the tawny owls have been very vocal recently. The only sound is of the breeze riffling through leaves of a black poplar and the trickling of the stream. The clouds thin and stars come out. A half-moon rises in the northeast. Stumbling blindly back through dark trees, the first orange street light opens the way to one life and closed the way back to another.

As a procession of cumulus cloud sails in from the southwest and a green woodpecker predicts the obvious, I walk across a field of recently harvested oilseed rape. I follow the hedge, under a landmark ash and around to a field corner I've never been to before. A charm of goldfinches bound over the hedge to reveal a view of Much Wenlock down the hill, rooftops buried in

trees. It's like being shown a vision from the distant past through a window: the gold of wheat and rye fields, the green of trees and pasture, the blue and silver sky.

Backlit by the sunset, the tall grasses of road verges and field headlands shine silver. The combine harvesters are working across the landscape, sucking up seas of wheat and barley. The orchids and hay rattle have seeds like coins in purses. Lime tree seeds, like tiny green versions of those brass balls which whiz round on steam engines but attached to a pale spinnaker bract, spiral down from branches. Unlike other seeds being produced now theirs will lie there uselessly, unable to germinate. The polished gold, copper and chocolate colours of many ripening seeds are picked up in the insignia of butterflies. On limestone grassland, gatekeeper and meadow browns are feeding on greater knapweed. In the woods, fritillaries sip from burdock in sunny rides.

From the top of Windmill Hill, surrounded by flowers of ladies bedstraw and eyebright, we watch as clouds drift in from the southwest. One, an agitated violet, lowers from a dark nest above the circle of hills surrounding Much Wenlock to cross the tops of trees. It ruptures and rains. The next morning, high cloud with blue slashes brings hope for a fine day. Sunny breaks are hot and humid. Paths up the steep side of the Edge are slick with mud and any depression holds a puddle. Wet clay, reaching bramble and the congealing green of the woods makes the going tougher. This is not the easy land it looks.

The old ways through this landscape: the packhorse tracks, cartways, footpaths, drover's roads and bridleways, have a logic to where they cross through the landscape, which is centuries old. Roman Bank is supposedly where the Romans quarried limestone slates to roof their city of Viraconium, now Wroxeter, 20 miles

Apedale from Upper Farm, Hatton

away and the hollow-ways used for transporting stone remain. Wenlock Edge is a natural barrier which makes coming and going difficult, and yet it is riddled with a network of tracks and small settlements.

On top of the Edge above Rushbury are hay meadows which seem to belong to the age of these ancient tracks, rather than having anything to do with modern agriculture. The sward is short, not much more than a foot in height, and full of wild flowers: seed cases of hay rattle, orchids, fescues and flickering now with ringlet and meadow brown butterflies. So few such meadows of traditional limestone grassland remain that these are not only of historic importance, they represent a reservoir of species to colonise restored grasslands of the future through conservation seed mixes. It is the survival of these flowery refuges which hold the future for many species of plants and insects.

A labyrinth of old ways leads through woods and fields, down to the castle mound which guards the approach to the village of Rushbury. On this grassy Norman motte, surrounded by a group of tups (rams), is an ancient ash tree; stumpy, broken and hollow, with huge bracket fungi and peppered with beetle and woodpecker holes; an entire nature reserve and living history in one tree, riddled with ancient ways with a logic of their own.

In recent years, summer has become the rainy season. Along quarry tops, where the green woodpecker goes, the wild flowers in rabbit-grazed turf are wonderful in summer: drifts of sweetly scented ladies bedstraw, tufty white patches of eyebright, pink scatterings of common centaury and restharrow, bright gold yellow-wort and St John's wort, dazzling pink pyramidal orchids, tatty rugs of wild thyme, sky-blue field scabious, resplendent purples of thistle, common and greater knapweed.

These plants are thriving but there's an odd silence where all the insects should be. I hope the woodpecker will still find plenty of ants, but even amongst all these flowers there is only one butterfly and there are far fewer of the scarlet and black five- and six-spot burnet moths. Where's the frantic fiddling of grasshoppers and crickets, the micro moths which scatter when you walk through long grass, the buzzing flies? Perhaps when the sun comes out for a little longer, the insects will too? Their wings hardly get the chance to dry out before another downpour soddens them again. This ominous silence does not bode well and the woodpecker forecasts rain.

A dark, piratical front of cloud, trailing black rags, sails low above and the feeling is like being in a Van der Graaf generator. If I had any hair it would stand on end. Instead I feel like a spinning compass which suddenly discovers a new pole. As the storm sails in, its underbelly is stroked by pink and orange light. Breathless, nothing moves and the world seems ghastly, beautiful, and profoundly ominous. It's obvious what is about to happen but that doesn't detract from the excitement when it does. As soon as the nuclear-orange glow fades, the first lightning strikes, then thunder rolls out from under the darkness, then it rains. And it rains and rains and rains. From the Edge, the River Severn can be seen spreading across its flood-plain; miles of land turned a strange orange colour.

Wildlife

By Caroline Uff

Nationally, many of the animals once familiar in the English countryside are becoming increasingly uncommon. However, here on the Edge there is a wealth of wildlife still to be found, thanks to the attractive mix of old and new habitats. The endearing Hazel Dormouse still thrives in the woodlands, whilst the arid open banks of the quarries are home to uncommon wild bees. Long forgotten creatures such as Glow-worms, Great Crested Newts, Slow-worms and fritillary butterflies still make their homes in the flower-rich meadows, shallow pools and shady lanes, just as they did a century ago.

Hazelnuts that have been nibbled by Dormice *(top)* and Woodmice *(bottom)* can be found in the autumn

Right: **Well-structured woodlands on Wenlock Edge offer an ideal habitat for Dormice**

Mammals and Other Vertebrates

The steep wooded slopes of Wenlock Edge, old quarries and surrounding farmland support a diverse range of wildlife. Of the mammals that are found here, the Dormouse population is particularly significant.

The Hazel Dormouse

Over the last 100 years, Dormouse populations in Britain have dramatically declined. In Shropshire, Dormice are thought to be near their most north-westerly limit in Europe, so they are particularly vulnerable, however there is a strong population on Wenlock Edge. The main reason for the national decline in Dormice is loss and fragmentation of habitat. Small isolated coppices may not be able to sustain healthy populations over long time periods. A Dormouse, being arboreal, is unlikely to cross open ground or even a long gap within a hedgerow. For this reason it is essential that continuous hedgerows are maintained offering safe links between woodlands, allowing populations to disperse.

- Dormice are small orange-brown mice with thick furry tails and black bulging eyes.
- They spend most of their life asleep, sleeping all day in the summer and hibernating from the end of October until April or even May.
- They are rarely seen because they are strictly nocturnal. They feed and nest in trees and shrubs and prefer not to come down to the ground.
- They live mostly in deciduous woodland and thick hedgerows feeding on nectar, fruits, nuts and insects.
- The easiest way of recognising sites used by Dormice is by finding characteristically gnawed hazelnuts. They leave perfectly round holes on the side of the shells with a virtually smooth inner rim. This distinguishes them from nuts eaten by other mice, voles and squirrels.
- Because of their rarity, Dormice are strictly protected by law. It is illegal to collect or knowingly disturb them in any way without a license from Natural England.

On wandering around Wenlock Edge woodland, it is clear that the management over past years has resulted in scattered areas of Hazel coppice amongst old mixed woodland. It has a varied structure with plenty of Honeysuckle and Bramble. All these provide an ideal habitat for Dormice. Searches for signs of Dormice activity show them to be present throughout the woodland. Wherever there is fruiting Hazel, it is likely that Dormouse-nibbled nuts will be found beneath.

Dormouse nests are typically found spun into the understorey of broadleaved woodland in summer; on Wenlock Edge Bramble is commonly used. The very distinctive nests are also made from neatly woven Honeysuckle bark. Grass may also be incorporated and

the outer layer made from carefully arranged leaves. A local forester recalls finding dormice many years ago in crevices of the quarry walls; recently they have also been shown to use conifers. However, boxes placed in conifer areas on Wenlock Edge have never been occupied, probably because there is more appropriate habitat nearby. During the winter months Dormice hibernate under tree roots.

National Trust monitors a series of Dormouse nest boxes in the woods. Most years, about 25% of the boxes show signs of use by Dormice, but it is rare to find a completely empty box. Often, in contrast to the neat nests of Dormice, nests of loose leaves are found which belong to Woodmice or Yellow-necked Mice. Birds (particularly tits) and bumblebees will also nest in the boxes whilst shrews and Copper Underwing Moths may be found sheltering. On the map of Dormouse distribution in Shropshire, Wenlock Edge clearly stands out as one of the county strongholds.

Dormouse distribution map

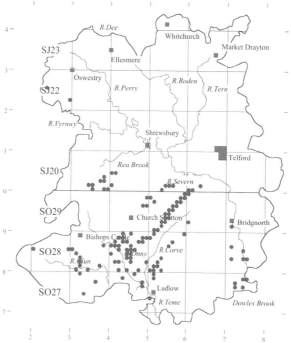

Left: Dormouse nest boxes are monitored each year

Middle: A typical Dormouse nest of woven Honeysuckle bark and leaves

Right: Honeysuckle is used by Dormice both for food and as a nesting material

Map courtesy of Alex Lockton

Other mammals

Other typical small woodland mammals known from the site include bats, Woodmice, Yellow-necked Mice, Bank Voles, rats and shrews. Field Voles are likely to be common in the more open areas and the uncommon Water Shrew has been recorded from Seifton Bache. Several suspected Harvest Mouse nests have been recently found in field boundaries; DNA testing is to be used to try and confirm whether this rare and treasured species is still present on the Edge.

Bats are known to be present along Wenlock Edge, they have not been surveyed in detail. However it seems likely that the Edge is of value as a breeding site as well as being an important foraging area. Brown Long-eared Bats have been found using Dormouse nest boxes in late spring. Old trees, disused tunnels and buildings have good potential to support hibernating bats whilst linear features such as the old railway track, hollow ways, hedgerows and paths are extremely important for navigation and forage. Natterer's Bats and Common Pipistrelle are known to use Wilderhope Manor and Lesser Horseshoe Bat roosts have recently been discovered by the Shropshire Bat Group in the area.

Of the larger mammals, the Badger, Fox, Polecat and Stoat are all found here. Brown Hare, a declining species nationally, are still often seen in the surrounding farmland as well as on the woodland rides. Otters have been recorded and are likely to occur in many of the streams draining the Edge. Otters suffered a massive decline nationally in the early 1960s, believed to be due to pollution and habitat loss. With improved water quality their numbers are now increasing.

Non-native mammals

There are several species of mammal found on the Edge that are not native to Britain. These include well-established species such as the Rabbit and Brown Rat as well as more recent introductions.

Fallow Deer and Muntjac are both known on Wenlock Edge but are not native. Deer in woodland are an accepted and often welcome part of UK biodiversity but mature deer have no natural predators. As a result, populations of most species are increasing and, in some areas of Britain, are causing damage to wild plant communities and crops. Fallow Deer are an early introduction and are present throughout most of England, although concentrated in the south and east. They are regularly seen on the Edge, but only in ones and twos. Muntjacs became established in the wild in the 1920s with their population centred on southeast and central England, but spreading west. Although Muntjac are rarely seen on the Edge, signs of them are present. One Roe buck has also been recorded on the Edge; it was probably just passing through but they are spreading quite quickly in the county. Currently the deer on Wenlock Edge are not causing significant damage to trees or coppice regeneration because their numbers are low. However, given the population trends, they are likely to increase and have an impact on the ecology of the area.

Another introduced species, the Grey Squirrel, is plentiful and was first introduced to England in the late 1800s. On Wenlock Edge they have caused problems with establishing trees, particularly young oaks. A squirrel may ringbark the upper parts of the tree or a single branch, particularly in early summer, causing these parts to die. Dead branches make good homes for many invertebrates and fungi, but are potentially

The roof voids of Wilderhope Manor are known to be home to maternity roosts of Common Pipistrelle and Brown Long-eared bats

Fallow deer tracks

Mink tracks,
front and rear

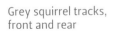

Grey squirrel tracks,
front and rear

dangerous for those involved in forestry operations. The native Red Squirrel was last recorded on the Edge in the 1950s.

American Mink were originally introduced to England for their fur in 1958 and have spread rapidly. They have been recorded in recent years from Wenlock Edge and have been seen in groups of up to a dozen. They are considerably smaller and darker than the native Otter.

Looking for tracks and signs such as nibbled hazelnuts, droppings or footprints in the mud is a great way to try and find out what mammals are present in the area.

Other vertebrates

The quarries are known to support a good population of Common Toad and Smooth Newt as well as the Great Crested Newt (a species which is legally protected). During the spring they use the quarry pools for breeding. Unlike frogs and toads, newt eggs are laid singly, folded into leaves of aquatic vegetation.

At other times of year the newts take refuge on land, under rocks or cracks in the quarry walls. Little is known about other vertebrates from the Edge, but Slow-worms and Common Lizards are occasionally seen. The Palmate Newt (typical of upland pools) and Common Frog have also been recorded from farmland and garden ponds in the area.

Male Smooth Newts develop a dorsal crest during the breeding season

Invertebrates

A wide and interesting range of invertebrates can be found in the woodlands, quarries and grasslands of Wenlock Edge. Species dependent on foliage, ancient trees, fungi, pools and open grassland habitats are all represented. Within the woodland, the more open conditions associated with the network of paths, rides and glades are far richer than the denser woodland. However it is the open quarry and grassland habitats that are most diverse. Invertebrates known from the area include a wide range of bees, wasps, dragonflies, hoverflies, beetles, robberflies, butterflies, snails and moths, some of which are nationally scarce or becoming increasingly uncommon.

Woodland insects

Right: **Moth trapping**

Below: **The longhorn beetle** *Rhagium bifisciatum* breeds in decaying conifer timber

Of significant interest are the invertebrates associated with dead wood, old boundary trees and fallen wood in the surrounding fields. They include around a dozen scarce or threatened species of false darkling beetles,

longhorn beetles, ground beetles, barkflies and solitary wasps. A recent survey found 13 species of bee and wasp that were dependant on the dead wood found along the woodland edge. Woodland fungi play an extremely important role not only in the decay process but also, in their own right, as home to a range of specialist invertebrates such as uncommon fungus beetles and gnats. The presence of all these species emphasise the importance of retaining standing and fallen dead wood and the careful management of ancient trees now and for the future.

The live foliage of trees, particularly native trees, is used by many invertebrates including leaf–roller weevils and other leaf beetles. Some trees will be so laden with moth caterpillars that on still days they can be heard moving and feeding amongst the leaves. On a typical summer night over 50 species of adult moth may come to a light trap. These include the Willow Beauty, July Highflier, Scalloped Oak, Buff Tip and Early Thorn moths. The larva of the Lunar Hornet Clearwing Moth feeds in the trunks and roots of large sallow trees.

The presence of distinctive exit holes (about the diameter of a pencil), can be found at the base of the trunk confirming the continued presence of this rarely seen species.

Some butterflies are also associated with the trees. The larvae of the declining White-letter Hairstreak feed on the elm trees of the Edge and Purple Hairstreak are associated with oak. Adults of these species are usually difficult to see as they fly high amongst the tree canopy feeding on honeydew. However, from the top of the scarp one can, in places, look down upon the treetops and may get a view of the adults flying around the oaks or elms below. Silver-washed Fritillary larvae feed on Common Dog-violet in shady conditions beneath; adults may be seen nectaring in the open glades or adjacent meadows.

Historically, the nationally-scarce Pearl-bordered Fritillary was recorded here but has not been seen since 1952. Like many of the woodland species mentioned, it was particularly associated with recently coppiced or cleared areas and open mosaics of woodland and grassland. Its decline coincided with the abandonment of the coppicing system and the planting of conifers between the 1940s and 1960s.

In recent years coppicing has been reintroduced and the conifer areas are steadily being reverted to broadleaf. The maintenance of wide rides and regular woodland management such as coppicing, ensures the continued

Silver-washed Fritillaries may be seen nectaring on Bramble

presence of open areas and a varied structure essential for a diverse woodland fauna.

Wide grassy rides like the disused railway track, with tall herb rich edges, provide an essential source of pollen and nectar for many woodland invertebrates. This is a particularly good place to find hoverflies such as the Snout Hoverfly *Rhingia rostrata*, the larva of which is believed to develop in badger dung. Many other flies such as tachanid flies that parasitise moth caterpillars and predacious robberflies are also found here. In the late summer, dragonflies can often be seen feeding along the rides, perhaps most frequently the red-coloured Common Darter. The damper areas of the ride host a variety of craneflies.

Above: Members of Shropshire Invertebrate Group in Lilleshall Quarry

Right: Solitary bee *Nomada leucophthalma*

Invertebrates of open grasslands and quarries

Areas of calcareous grassland and open sunny banks, associated with rock outcrops and quarry workings, offer an excellent habitat for warmth-loving invertebrates. Numerous solitary mining bees and wasps can be seen going in and out of nesting holes along these banks. The solitary bees create these holes to lay their eggs and then provide their young with pollen and nectar. Others are described as 'cuckoos' and, like the bird, they lay their eggs in the nests of other bees. Solitary wasps may also live in holes in the ground, but most of those recorded on the site nest in dead wood. They hunt invertebrates such as flies, aphids and spiders, which they use as a food supply for their developing young.

In recent surveys, 81 different species of bee and wasp were found, most of which were associated with the south-facing open banks and sparsely vegetated grassland of Lea Quarry. The limestone flora provides a diverse nectar and pollen source, most of the species recorded forage from a variety of flowers. Some of the species are known to be of national importance including *Arachnospila minutula*, a spider-hunting wasp and *Stelis ornatula*, a cuckoo of a deadwood nesting bee. Another interesting species is *Tiphia minuta*, a solitary wasp that parasitizes the larva of dung beetles.

The sparsely vegetated areas around the quarries are also important for several nationally-declining butterfly and moth species, including strong populations of Wall Brown and Small Heath butterflies.

Several small populations of the declining Dingy Skipper and Brown Argus butterflies have recently been discovered in the disused quarries. Green Hairstreak and Cinnabar Moths are also present on the quarry edge, whilst the purple and gold day-flying pyralid moth *Pyrausta aurata* can be seen in good numbers

around herb rich banks. The immigrant Hummingbird Hawkmoth is a day flying moth that is seen most years here, typically hovering in front of flowers, sipping the nectar with its long proboscis.

It is important for these species that the habitat is kept open. Quarrying is an ideal way to keep a succession of open areas, but in areas where quarrying is no longer going on, scrub clearing supported by grazing prevents them from becoming overgrown. The policy of tree planting used by many quarries is controversial from an ecological viewpoint as it would be detrimental to the invertebrate fauna of this area.

Some of the larger areas of grassland, such as Ippikin's Meadow and the meadows at the northern end of Blakeway Hollow also support a wide range of invertebrates. The fauna is at its richest before the meadows are cut for hay, when bees and butterflies abound. Common and widespread species include the Meadow Brown, Gatekeeper, Small Skipper and Common Blue butterfly. Common Carder, Red-tailed and White-tailed Bumblebees are frequent, grasshoppers chirp

constantly in the background and on summer nights Glow-worms can be seen. Anthills of the Yellow Meadow Ant are found here, particularly on small old meadows such as the Pudding Bag at Wilderhope. Their presence reflects the lack of recent agricultural improvement, particularly ploughing. On closer inspection, a wealth of other invertebrates is apparent. Many, such as the Six-belted Clearwing moth and solitary bee *Lasioglossum malachurum*, are becoming increasingly uncommon in the country as their habitat is lost.

The diverse habitats found on Wenlock Edge, including ancient broadleaved woodland, flower-rich hay meadows and open quarry grassland are all increasingly rare habitats. They are vital to the rich and treasured range of animals which live here and need to be carefully managed for future generations to enjoy.

Above: Anthills in Pudding Bag at Wilderhope are indicative of ancient pasture

Left: Dingy Skippers can be found in grasslands which contain their foodplant Bird's-foot Trefoil

Right: Brown Argus

Top left: Gatekeeper butterfly
Above: Dock Shieldbug nymph
Far left: Green Shieldbug with eggs
Left: Cinnabar Moth caterpillars
Below: Speckled Wood butterfly
Opposite, top left: Solitary bee *Andrena clarkella*
Top right: Swollen–thighed Beetle
Bottom left: Wall Brown butterfly
Bottom right: Grasshopper

Birds

By Leo Smith

Birds are an integral part of the atmosphere of a wander along any part of the Edge, especially in spring and early summer. The song of residents like Robins and Blackbirds, the melodies of the warblers that come for the summer, the drumming of woodpeckers, the ringing call of Nuthatches to proclaim their territories and the 'cronking' Ravens and mewing Buzzards overhead, all contribute to an enjoyable day out.

Readers not familiar with all the birds described in this chapter are recommended to invest in a good field guide.

Habitat on the Edge

Resident birds need to be able to find food all year, but they, together with the summer migrants, need an abundance between May and July when they are raising families. At this time the birds mainly feed on invertebrates: worms, caterpillars and other insects, so a diverse range of plant species, trees of different ages and dead wood are all required to host these invertebrates.

However, much of the woodland along the Edge is young and dense. It was mainly planted in compartments in the 1950s, in many places it provides little variety in either tree species or age. Management in recent years has been limited to conifer removal, coppicing and ride-side work, so in most parts of the wood the understorey is largely overgrown and the canopy overhead is closed. Most of the trees have smooth trunks and little rough broken bark, with few nooks and crannies where insects can flourish. This type of woodland limits the variety and number of birds.

The Trust has embarked on a new long-term management plan, aiming to rectify this limitation by increasing the diversity of woodland species and structure. Large areas will be eventually restored to Ancient Semi-natural Woodland. This increase in woodland diversity is intended, over many years, to slowly but steadily improve the habitat for a variety of woodland birds, thereby hopefully increasing their populations.

The absence of trees with holes has been addressed by starting a nest box scheme.

The minor road from Corvedale to Longville effectively splits the Edge in two. Much of the woodland to the south of that is more diverse and open; closer to Craven Arms the continuous line of woodland is broken where it has been cleared for farmland. There are more oak woods at the southern end, with plantations of conifers, including Strefford Wood, owned by the Forestry Commission.

Mature oak trees in particular provide excellent bird habitat. They support the greatest number of invertebrates, particularly large numbers of caterpillars, often having dead branches and naturally occurring holes.

Most birds nesting in woodland can be divided into seven groups, those that:

- Build nests on or close to the ground, hidden in the undergrowth, such as the commonest resident birds (Wren, Dunnock, Robin and Blackbird), the warblers and the increasingly rare Woodcock
- Build nests in forks or on top of branches, well off the ground, such as Sparrowhawk, Wood Pigeon, Carrion Crow and Chaffinch
- Nest inside naturally occurring holes, such as Marsh, Blue and Great Tits and Pied Flycatcher
- Nest in crevices between broken bark and tree trunks, such as Treecreeper
- Excavate their own nest holes, such as Great Spotted Woodpecker and Willow Tit
- Modify existing holes, either naturally occurring or previously made by woodpeckers, such as Nuthatch
- Favour particular tree species, in the way that Coal Tits and Goldcrests utilise conifers

Most birds in the first two categories can nest anywhere along the Edge, the limiting factor on their populations being food supply.

For the other birds, most of the trees are not mature enough, or are of the wrong species to have many naturally occurring nest holes, or much dead wood and other habitat for insects. Therefore the different woodland structures support vastly different numbers of the birds in the third category, while the Treecreeper is found in very few places.

Although Great Spotted Woodpeckers prefer making holes in dead trees, they are widespread, as they are strong enough to excavate a hole in most trees. However, the much smaller Willow Tits can only utilise either dead wood, or soft coniferous wood, thus they are rare. Conifers do not occur naturally along the Edge, but where they do now occur Goldcrests are more likely to be found in their vicinity.

Some of the larger birds, such as Buzzard, Red Kite and especially Raven require large trees to support heavy nests; they also need an open aspect, so they can fly in and out easily and their young can fledge safely while their aerobatic skills are undeveloped. Such trees are in short supply on many parts of the Edge itself, although they are more common in some of the adjacent woods. Ravens favour the larger conifers, particularly Scots Pine, especially where they are on the edge of the wood, or immediately next to it. Such trees provide sturdy branches and evergreen cover, both of which provide additional security and protection from the hard winter weather, in the early part of the nesting period between February and May.

In addition to favouring particular types and ages of the trees, some woodland birds also require specific types of understorey: for example, Redstarts need short ground vegetation for feeding; Wood Warblers need a low understorey and open areas under the canopy for their display flight; Woodcocks need wet ground for feeding near dry ground with sparse cover for nesting. These needs are rarely met along most of the Edge.

Great Spotted Woodpecker

The Edge also includes another important habitat; rock faces in natural cliffs and quarries, together with open spaces around the quarries. Wheatears breed here. The ledges on the rock faces also provide nest and roost sites for Stock Doves and Jackdaws, as well as for some of the birds of prey and Ravens, described later. The future management of these sites, now the quarrying has ceased and scrub is regenerating, will have a major impact on the number and variety of bird species that you can find.

Woodland birds

The resident woodland birds include the tits, woodpeckers, Nuthatch and Treecreeper. Many of the more common, less specialised species, such as Wren, Dunnock, Robin, Blackbird and Chaffinch also nest in the woods along the Edge. This chapter concentrates on the less common birds that mainly inhabit woodland, largely ignoring the more common and widespread species which can also be found in suburban gardens.

In summer the residents are joined by migrants, particularly the warblers, such as Chiffchaff and Blackcap.

For most song bird species, only the males sing, doing so to attract a mate and defend a breeding territory. For most of the day they do this sporadically, every male starting the day with a short burst of sustained song. All the different songs can be heard together and be picked out like the different instruments in a large orchestra. Everyone interested in nature and wildlife should experience the 'dawn chorus' at least once in their lives.

Once the need for the males to sing is over (when the females are sitting on the final clutch of eggs) the Edge becomes much quieter. However, there is still a lot of activity as birds are conspicuous when gathering food for young nestlings; family parties with recently fledged young are also very noticeable, especially as the contact calls which keep the family together draw attention to them. When the young become independent, spending all their time foraging for themselves, the parents take a well-earned rest and woods become very quiet, seeming devoid of birds from early July onwards.

Resident birds tend to raise one brood. Eggs are laid in April or early May and incubated for around two weeks. The nestlings fledge around two to three weeks after hatching. In general, the larger birds have longer incubation and fledging periods. The summer migrants more commonly lay in mid May, raising two broods.

All of these species, except the increasingly rare Woodcock, should be found in May.

Woodcock

Woodcocks are specialist woodland wading birds, and need wet ground together with open glades and rides for breeding. They are crepuscular (active mainly at dawn and dusk), nesting in sparse cover on the ground. The dominant colour of their superb cryptic camouflage is the same as dead leaf litter, so they remain well hidden during the day and are only seen if they are flushed. The best chance of seeing one is at dusk, by finding a vantage point with extensive views of suitable breeding habitat, then watching for the male's distinctive 'roding' display flight.

The small breeding population is supplemented in winter by a large influx of birds from the woodlands of northern Europe. They escape to the Edge when the ground in the woods where they breed freezes over and they are unable to feed.

Treecreeper

Tits

All six members of the tit family that breed in England are found on the Edge, but Marsh Tit and Willow Tit are encountered less that the other four. These two tits are very similar and they are best separated by their characteristic calls; a good view is necessary to separate them by sight, even then it is not always possible. Marsh Tits are generally much smarter and neater; the head is shiny black and the bib much smaller and square. Willow Tits are more scruffy and bulky, especially the neck which needs to be strong; they are the only British tit to excavate its own nest hole. The head appears to be a dull black because in fact it is dark chocolate brown. However, there is overlap in the physical characteristics between these two species, and the only certain difference is in some of the calls.

Woodpeckers

Great Spotted is the most common woodpecker and is likely to be seen on most visits. Nationally the population has more than quadrupled since 1970, including a doubling in the last 15 years or so. An increase in food, in dead timber caused by Dutch Elm Disease, probably facilitated the first surge; milder winters, together with an increase in food found in maturing plantations and at garden bird tables, fuelled the more recent surge.

Green Woodpeckers mainly feed on ants, especially Wood Ants in conifers, but they forage on any uncultivated open ground. They excavate nest holes in soft or dead wood, so the young age of the woodland and the extensive undergrowth on most parts of the Edge will restrict breeding opportunities. However, these woodpeckers do breed near Lea Quarry, where grazing of the newly created grassland provides good feeding areas of short turf. They can also be found where there

are large stands of coniferous woods. Milder winters will have benefited this woodpecker too, but it is unlikely that the habitat here provides enough food to support a large increase in the population.

Lesser Spotted Woodpeckers are tiny, only the size of House Sparrows, usually making their nest hole in the underside of a decaying branch. There are unlikely to be many on the Edge because the trees are unsuitable. If they are seen, this is much more likely to be in oak wood nearby, or on alders along the streams, rather than on the Edge itself, except perhaps at the southern end.

Nuthatch and Treecreeper

These are closely related species, but they look and behave very differently, although they both feed on insects on the trunks and branches of trees.

Nuthatches have a sturdy pointed bill and are the only birds that will be seen walking down branches and tree trunks, pecking hard as they go to open up the bark to find food. The loud tapping is often the first clue that they are around. They nest in old holes, sometimes using ones made by Great Spotted Woodpeckers, plastering the entrance with mud to reduce the size of the hole and protect themselves from predators.

Treecreepers have a relatively long curved beak which they use to probe the cracks in the bark as they move up the tree. When they get to the top they fly down to the base of the next tree and start their upward foraging climb all over again.

On the Edge the woodland is much less suitable for Treecreepers than Nuthatches, so the latter are more common.

Willow Tit

Marsh Tit

Goldcrest

Nuthatch

Chiffchaff

Willow Warbler

Blackcap

Wood Warbler

Summer Migrants

The resident birds are supplemented by migrants that come here to breed. Several warblers which winter in Africa are common in spring and summer adding to the symphony of song. They are all smaller than a House Sparrow, and are usually seen feeding on insects while flitting around the tree tops. They all build nests in the undergrowth, on or close to the ground. They mostly start breeding later than the resident birds, but often raise two broods.

Chiffchaff is named after its monotonous song, which is one of the easiest to remember and recognise. It is mainly a dull olive green, with an indistinct stripe just above the eye. It is amongst the first summer visitors to arrive, in mid–March, being announced by the song, usually from the tops of tall trees.

Willow Warbler, with a descending cascade of notes, again usually sung from the tree tops, is one of the most common of our birds, arriving from mid–April onwards. It looks very similar to Chiffchaff and is usually separated from it by the song.

Blackcap is less common and more skulking. It has a more melodious and explosive song, one of the most beautiful heard in Britain, usually from deep within undergrowth and tall bushes, rather than the trees. Both sexes are a uniform grey-brown above and paler olive–grey below, except for the cap on the top of the head; males have a black cap, but females and juveniles have one of chestnut brown.

Garden Warbler is the least common. Its colouration and behaviour is similar to the Blackcap, their songs are very similar too. However, the Garden Warbler has no cap; it is usually described as having no distinguishing features at all. Knowing this may not be much help, as it is even harder to get a good view.

Several other summer visitors that inhabit woodland: Tree Pipit, Wood Warbler, Redstart, Spotted Flycatcher and Pied Flycatcher are found in the area, but they are not very common along the Edge itself.

However, the old buildings and open ground around the quarries provide nest sites and feeding areas for the colourful Redstart; the male has a grey crown and back, white forehead and black head and throat, both sexes having a bright red tail which shivers when they land. The Lime Kilns at Presthope provide good breeding habitat for Spotted flycatchers, where they perch on exposed branches in clearings and dash out to catch flying insects, flying back to the same perch or a similar one nearby. They nest in recesses on tree trunks or in walls, often hidden by climbing shrubs.

Above: **Redstart**
Below: **Spotted Flycatcher**

Sparrowhawk

Birds of prey & Ravens

You will encounter the woodland birds described above most frequently, but seeing and hearing one of the birds of prey, or a Raven, on the Edge, is a special thrill not to be forgotten.

Several of these birds are present now for the first time in well over a hundred years, others having a much higher population than they did 50 years ago. They were largely wiped out by human persecution during the 19th Century, their slow recovery in the 20th Century was reversed by indirect poisoning by agricultural chemicals such as DDT. These poisons built up to fatal levels in the body fat of adult birds, their breeding success was also seriously reduced. As use of these chemicals was controlled and steadily reduced from the 1960s onwards, the populations of these raptors returned to previous levels. However, direct poisoning and shooting by gamekeepers and, to a lesser extent farmers, also held back the recovery until legislative protection introduced in 1981 was actually enforced from the 1990s onwards.

The population increases of Sparrowhawk, Peregrine, Buzzard, Red Kite and Raven and their presence now along the Edge, are major conservation success stories, highlighting the importance of monitoring population change in bird species at the top of the food chain, to assess the impact of human activities on the natural environment.

Sparrowhawk

Sparrowhawks are the specialist woodland raptors, dashing through the trees and feeding on small birds caught in flight, mainly in glades and clearings inside the wood, or along nearby hedgerows. They are extremely manoeuvrable in the enclosed spaces, being more than willing to crash into a bush in pursuit of a fleeing quarry. They are now undoubtedly the most common bird of prey along the Edge, as they spend most of their time inside the wood they are therefore rarely seen.

Goshawk

Goshawks are like big Sparrowhawks but are even more elusive, rarely leaving large woods. They are still heavily persecuted by gamekeepers and nests are robbed by falconers. The British population was estimated at only 400 pairs in 1995, so these fast and powerful raptors are seen very rarely.

Kestrel

You are most likely to be rewarded by the sight of a Kestrel, the most conspicuous of the small raptors, easily recognised by its characteristic hovering flight before diving to catch prey on the ground, giving rise to one of the ancient names for the species, 'Windhover'.

Kestrels are resident along the Edge, favouring hunting areas over open ground. This includes the quarries; the path overlooking Lea Quarry is a good place to see them from. Their most common prey is the Short-tailed Field Vole, this diet is supplemented with other small rodents and birds. They may be seen at any time of the year, even in severe winter conditions.

Most nests here are on cliffs or crags, or in old crow's nests. Both males and females can be seen hunting in April, but females are rarely seen once they start incubating, usually at the beginning of May, until they start hunting again several weeks later to help feed well-grown young in the nest. Family parties of up to six might be seen hovering in July, all well spaced out, and facing into the wind.

They are probably the most common bird of prey in Britain and in Shropshire, although the woodland Sparrowhawk is more common along the Edge itself.

Peregrine

You may be lucky enough to hear a loud thud overhead, looking up to see a shower of feathers floating down and a Peregrine carrying off its prey, caught in mid air. Pigeons and Jackdaws are the favourite food here, these raptors taking almost any medium sized bird that they can catch in flight.

They are most commonly seen soaring, or almost stationary in the air, floating into the wind. They are most conspicuous when displaying in March or early April, or with fledged young in July and August, but they might be seen at any time. Adult birds stay in the breeding territory all year, except in very hard conditions, but most juveniles go to the estuaries for winter.

Peregrines usually nest on rock ledges on cliffs; they took advantage of a big increase in available nest sites in the quarries made in the post-war period by the construction industry. They have continued to increase, and are now more common in Britain than they have ever been. The first ever nest recorded in Shropshire was found in the south-west as recently as 1987, but the County population has now grown to over 20 pairs.

Some of the quarries and cliffs along the Edge may provide suitable nest sites.

Peregrines are still persecuted by egg collectors, falconers and pigeon fanciers, in spite of this being illegal, so nest sites are kept confidential.

Buzzard

You are now likely to see several Buzzards during a walk along the Edge, soaring effortlessly on rising thermals, or passing over on the way to their foraging areas in the surrounding countryside. Buzzards are the most common of the larger birds of prey. Most nests are built in the larger deciduous trees and completed in late April. One or two young usually fledge from each of the successful nests in July; family parties can then be seen soaring together anywhere along the Edge.

Buzzards almost became extinct in Shropshire at the end of the 19th Century. The population slowly increased and spread until the 1950s, when myxomatosis wiped out most of their staple diet of rabbits, it then crashed by about 75%, after which it has slowly increased again. Shropshire was a national black spot for illegal shooting and poisoning of birds of prey up until the 1990s, Buzzards being the main victim. However, they have benefited from more recent enforcement of the legislative protection and from an improved food supply; an increase in sheep carrion since the early 1990s and an increase in the rabbit

Kestrel

population following recovery from myxomatosis. As a result, the local population has increased considerably in recent years; their breeding density has increased and their range has also expanded out of the uplands, so they may now be seen anywhere in Shropshire. The recovery of the Buzzard is undoubtedly a recent conservation success story.

Red Kite

Red Kites are the most graceful of Britain's birds of prey. You might see them anywhere, drifting over the treetops as they spread along the Edge from the south-western end, near Craven Arms. Their wing span is greater than a Buzzard, they are more brightly coloured and more lightly built, so their flight is more buoyant. They are best distinguished by the long forked red tail, which they twist from side to side for balance and direction in flight.

Kites almost became extinct in Britain as a result of ruthless and sustained human persecution. Only a few pairs were left in the hills of mid Wales by the early 1930s, for several years only a single female produced a chick. The whole fate of the native population hung on this one bird, a really close call. Numbers slowly increased, assisted by systematic and intensive conservation work, finally reaching 100 pairs by 1993. Since then the population grew much more rapidly, their range has also expanded from their stronghold in the central Cambrian Mountains, near Tregaron and Rhayader. There are now almost certainly over 1,000 breeding pairs in Wales.

The Welsh population has spilled over the border, as the South Shropshire Hills provides excellent habitat; Red Kites have been seen increasingly frequently since the turn of the century. Young birds wander widely and cover large distances very quickly while looking for food, so most of these sightings will be of immature birds. Around 33% die

Red Kite

in their first year, but after that the annual survival rate is around 80%, some birds living to 20 years old, or longer.

Two pairs of kites nested in Shropshire in 2005, the first known in the County since 1876. Both were unsuccessful, but one pair fledged two young in 2006, the first successful breeding for 130 years. The Shropshire population has expanded rapidly since then, 20 nests were found in 2011. Breeding success has also been higher than the average in Wales so the county population is expected to continue to increase and spread.

Their main food is young rabbits and voles during the summer and worms and carrion during the winter. They feed their young in the nest with live prey, particularly young crows and Magpies. Since 1989 reintroduction programmes have also taken place in several parts of England and Scotland. These populations have also increased and spread, so some birds from them are also reaching here and may be seen along the Edge.

Kites might be seen any time of year, but they are most conspicuous while prospecting for potential breeding sites in March and April, then again during post-breeding dispersal in August to October. They are very shy and may desert their nest if they are disturbed. They still suffer from egg collecting, so they are legally protected and nest sites are kept strictly confidential.

Raven

The Raven's loud, far carrying 'cronk' call, often accompanied by a tumbling display flight, is the most evocative sound of the hills in late winter and early spring. The pair wheel and soar together, their flight so synchronised that the wings appear to be joined at the tips. Pairs are very territorial and nests are widely spaced, so the population is still small, although it is increasing rapidly. The Raven population in Shropshire was estimated at only 30 to 35 pairs in 1990, almost all in the south-west hills, with only one possible breeding pair anywhere along the whole Edge. By 1999 there were several known nests along the Edge and numbers have continued to increase. Raven nests might be found anywhere where there are suitable cliffs, quarry faces or large trees. There are now several hundred pairs in Shropshire. The Edge provides excellent habitat, there are now probably around 10 breeding pairs along the Edge or in nearby woods.

Ravens are omnivorous and mainly eat carrion. The population growth is attributed mainly to a better food supply, due to an increase in carrion left lying around in the uplands. Sheep carcasses used to be removed and taken to the knackers yard but the financial incentive for this disappeared, (the Government having changed the regulations governing the use of materials reclaimed from carcasses, to combat the spread of BSE in the early 1990s). This carrion supply is supplemented at the height of the breeding season by dead lambs and afterbirth, produced by the practice of lambing out on the hillsides. Increased winter food supply from dead pheasants and road kill, together with milder winters and reduction in illegal poisoning, have also reduced annual mortality rates.

Ravens breed very early. The nest is usually completed by early February and most females will be incubating before the end of the month. The most commonly observed evidence of an active nest is seeing Ravens noisily drive off other predatory birds, particularly Buzzards. Family parties may be seen any time from early May onwards. Breeding is timed to coincide with the lambing season and Ravens are considered to be nature's refuse collectors.

Half of all young Ravens die before they are fourteen months old, mortality continues to be high until the few remaining birds become established in breeding pairs, usually when they are around three years old. Once they acquire territories, breeding birds may live until they are 10 years old, or longer. Because many young birds need to be born to ensure that enough of them reach breeding age, there are almost as many immature birds, three years old or less, than there are adult breeding birds. Small flocks and occasionally much larger ones can be seen all over the Shropshire Hills.

Population change

The preceding descriptions of the woodland birds, and the birds of prey and Raven, show that bird populations are not static, but change rapidly to reflect changes in their environment. For migrant species, these changes may occur thousands of miles away. Some of these changes occur naturally, but most are directly or indirectly the result of human activity:

- Persecution – by shooting, trapping and poisoning
- Agricultural change – including use of farm chemicals with unknown side effects
- Increasing the food supply for carrion eaters, particularly through sheep farming and pheasant shooting
- Development – for example, new homes, offices, retail parks and countryside recreational facilities, which all take an increasing amount of land
- Recreation – increased walking for leisure, especially with dogs, which increases disturbance, particularly at nesting time when birds are most vulnerable
- Habitat destruction – through active management, felling of woodlands, or no management at all
- Introduction of alien species – deer and Grey Squirrel have a major impact on woodland habitats
- Changing land use in the winter quarters of migrant birds – using water for irrigation, drainage, and an increase in grazing, especially by goats
- The various impacts of climate change, both here and in sub-saharan Africa

All these activities can have a drastic, sometimes devastating effect on the well-being of particular species. In some cases declines have been recognised and reversed through active conservation and protection. The British population of Peregrine Falcon is probably the highest it has ever been, Red Kite and Buzzard are at their highest numbers for over 150 years. Although the numbers of many of the resident woodland birds are increasing, the populations of many species found on the Edge have declined considerably in recent years. Conservation action is being taken to try and reverse these losses.

Winter thrushes

Fieldfares and Redwings, about a million of each, come to Britain for the winter. The Fieldfares mainly come from Scandinavia, but Redwings come from both there and Iceland. Both have characteristic chattering calls (the Fieldfare is much louder), so finding the flocks is easy. They usually contain both species and often include our native thrushes as well.

Other winter visitors that might be seen around the foothills are Bramblings, close relatives of Chaffinches. Most of them also come from Scandinavia, but some come from as far east as the Urals. They feed on beech mast, so the number coming to Britain depends on its abundance, which fluctuates from year to year.

The Crossbill population also increases in the winter. These birds feed on the seeds in pine cones, which their beaks are specially adapted to extract. Like Bramblings, the numbers that come each year fluctuate, depending on the availability of food closer to home. However, Crossbills do breed in Shropshire in small numbers, and they may be found in the coniferous woods on the Edge at any time of year. Similarly, Siskins breed locally in small numbers, mainly in the conifers; numbers also increase with an influx of winter visitors. Their diet is less specialised, and they can be found eating Alder seeds and commonly at garden feeders with peanuts.

Where to go

There is a wide variation in the tree species and in the age and structure of woodlands along the Edge, which in turn affects the variation and numbers of the birds to be found in different places. If you want to see and hear a good variety of birds you need to plan your walk carefully. Those who want to see the birds as well as hear them need to be even more selective. There are few places where there is an extensive view through the trees, or large patches of sky visible overhead. Those paths that traverse the middle of steep slopes do give good views into the canopy of the trees on the downhill side.

Many birds forage in several different habitats, looking for different foods in each, so woodland edge and large clearings provide both the greatest variety of species and the best views. Perhaps the best areas are: the route to Blakeway Coppice along the bottom of the wood, starting at the foot of Harley Bank on the A458 Much Wenlock to Shrewsbury road; the path overlooking Lea Quarry, walking north-east from the

Fieldfare

Male Siskin

Wenlock Edge car park at Presthope; the varied section of woodland and scrub at the highest point of the road from Longville to Wilderhope; and the open and diverse woodland between Wilderhope and Roman Bank.

Good views of many of the birds can be obtained from a hide, near Presthope. Nest boxes and a feeding station ensure their continuous presence. Bird ringing demonstrations are also held there.

Recommended walk

Apart from the best areas on the Edge itself, listed above, the best walk for birds probably starts at Wilderhope Manor. Walking round the Manor building and scanning the farmyard before following the Wilderhope Coppice path, at least as far as the pool, adds several additional species to those likely to be seen on the Edge itself. Swallows nest in the porches of both entrances to the Manor building; Swifts nest under the eaves and under the large flagstones making up the roof. The farm buildings provide nest sites for House Sparrow (unusual along the Edge) and perhaps Collared Dove.

The hedgerows along the track to the pool hold Whitethroat and Yellowhammer, while the mature oak trees just before the pool are more open than most places on the Edge itself, providing a much better range of caterpillars and other invertebrates (bird food), also affording better views of many of the woodland specialities like Spotted Flycatcher, Nuthatch and Treecreeper (which also like the Alders by the stream).

The small pool holds breeding Mallard, Tufted Duck, Canada Goose, Little Grebe, Moorhen and Coot.

Continuing towards Wrens Nest, then bearing right into the wood along the Wilderhope Coppice Walk, pass

Wilderhope Manor

through some excellent mixed woodland, including oak trees. The track steadily rises, and then splits into two.

The left fork, marked Corvedale, goes up to the crest and there is a particularly good stretch of wood and woodland edge at the highest point. The path continues south-west along the crest of Stanway Coppice (always keep left, with the woodland edge in view on the left, at any path junction in the wood) and then crosses onto farmland but continues along the woodland edge, then down hill almost as far as Hopes Cross. Towards the bottom of the hill, when the farm buildings in Corvedale are close, cut back right through the gate (footpath marker on top of the gatepost, not very visible), then down to the stream and back to the Manor past Lower

Stanway. The Alders, coppice and scrub along the stream provide excellent habitat for warblers and Treecreeper, while the farm buildings at Lower Stanway add House Martin and Pied Wagtail to the species list. This gives a varied circular walk of around four miles (six kilometres) which should yield around 40 species in summer, and 30 in winter. The walking takes a bit less than two hours, so allowing three hours or more gives plenty of time to look and listen for the birds.

The right fork, signed Wilderhope Coppice Walk, goes back down through the wood and is described fully in the National Trust walks leaflet. The habitats are not so varied, being mainly woodland and open farmland, so the bird species list will not be as great, but the route is much shorter (allow 45 minutes for the walk, plus another hour to look for the birds); it will still give good opportunities to see most of the woodland birds.

At the beginning or end of the walk, a detour of 250 metres along the footpath north-north-eastwards from Wilderhope Manor, signposted to Much Wenlock, followed by a right turn, arrives near a large pool (only dug recently, so not shown on older Ordnance Survey maps), which often provides better views of the water birds found on the small pool, and also Mute Swan and Greylag Goose, in April to June.

The increasingly threatened Lapwing might be found breeding just south of Longville and in the vicinity of Wilderhope Farm, if spring crops have been planted.

Another good area to walk, with diverse woodlands and birds, is around Harton Hollow car park, on the top of the ridge north of Westhope and south of Harton (OS Grid Reference SO 480 876). Harton Hollow itself is a Shropshire Wildlife Trust nature reserve, with interesting geology and plants.

Harton Hollow

Species list

The best time to look and listen for birds along the Edge is undoubtedly the first half of May. Most birds are most active in the morning, so the earlier in the day the better.

A circular walk along the crest, taking in the path along the top of Lea Quarry, and returning along the woodland edge at the bottom of the escarpment, should find most of the following species (listed in Field Guide order): Sparrowhawk, Buzzard, Kestrel, Peregrine, Stock Dove, Woodpigeon, Collared Dove, Great Spotted Woodpecker, Green Woodpecker, Wren, Dunnock, Robin, Wheatear*, Blackbird, Song Thrush, Blackcap*, Garden Warbler*, Chiffchaff*, Willow Warbler*, Goldcrest, Long-tailed Tit, Blue Tit, Great Tit, Coal Tit, Willow Tit, Marsh Tit, Spotted Flycatcher*, Nuthatch, Treecreeper, Jay, Magpie, Jackdaw, Carrion Crow, Raven, House Sparrow, Tree Sparrow, Chaffinch, Greenfinch, Goldfinch, Linnet and Bullfinch.

Extending the walk through adjacent farmland, hills and dales, including visiting some of the local oak woods and pools, or taking the recommended walk from Wilderhope Manor, should add most of the following species: Canada Goose, Mallard, Red-legged Partridge, Pheasant, Little Grebe, Grey Heron, Red Kite, Moorhen, Coot, Lapwing, Cuckoo*, Tawny Owl, Swift*, Skylark, Swallow*, House Martin*, Pied Wagtail, Redstart*, Mistle Thrush, Whitethroat*, Rook, Starling and Yellowhammer.

Taking the detour 250 metres along the footpath north-north-eastwards from Wilderhope Manor to the large pool should add: Mute Swan, Greylag Goose and Tufted Duck.

There is also a chance of finding several more rare woodland species, though they are more likely to be found in adjacent woods, rather than along the Edge itself: Woodcock, Lesser Spotted Woodpecker, Tree Pipit*, Wood Warbler*, Pied Flycatcher* and Redpoll.

Though most birds are less conspicuous in June, a visit at this time to Wilderhope Manor and the pools provides spectacular compensations: family parties of screaming Swifts swirling around the Manor House, Swallows and House Martins skimming the surface of the pool to catch insects, and charms of Goldfinches.

The species marked with an asterisk * are summer migrants, which only come here for the breeding season. The others are resident birds, which are supplemented in winter by several different migrant visitors mainly from October onwards, such as: Lesser Black-backed Gull, Fieldfare, Redwing, Brambling, Siskin and Crossbill.

The small resident population of Woodcock is also supplemented by a large number of winter visitors.

FIELD GUIDES

The RSPB has produced two field guides, the simple *RSPB Pocket Guide to British Birds* (Harrap) covers 174 species, and the more informative and detailed *RSPB Handbook of British Birds* (Holden and Cleeves), covering 280 species.

If you want a Guide that covers all European birds, *Collins Bird Guide* (Mullarney, Svensson, Zetterstrom and Grant 2001), published by Harper Collins, is currently reputed to be the best.

A selection of other good field guides are widely available.

Above Midddlehope at dusk

Landscape & Seasons:
Autumn

Autumn slips in under moonlight. A big silver moon, with a quarter sliced from its northern side, swings high into the night sky with a swirl of clouds around it the colour of lead ore.

The clouds spread, separate, organise themselves into a long reptilian pattern glowing pale, pressed flat against the blue–black sky as if hammered out of aluminium.

In the morning the sky is milky grey and wet. There's a special quality to the sounds of rain in autumn trees. Under tall oaks and limes, when a breeze ruffles the topmost branches, there is a long pouring of raindrops through the canopy, like handfuls of opals plunging over leaves. Under smaller hawthorns and field maples, the percussive splatterings create a more intimate, dripping-cave kind of environment. Where there is no detracting light and the horizon is hidden, even from the hills, sounds carry the invisible qualities of the landscape.

Walking in woods, through scrub, on open pasture, between hedges and fields and along tree-lined avenues, there is a diverse aural topography of rain which picks out the forms and structures in the landscape, through the sounds of raindrops falling through them. There are other evocative sounds too; the calls of crows sketch out the middle distance in strong dark strokes like charcoal. The subdued songs of blackbirds and robins cross-hatch the rain-made shapes of the immediate and reachable. In this myopic but sound-induced landscape things present themselves that may otherwise be missed: the curious vocalisation of a raven flying past, making a grunting sound which ends in a high-pitched hiccup; the berries of dogwood, held upright from purpling leaves are as shiny-black as the pupils of birds eyes; the huge horizontal bough of the horse chestnut tree which defied gravity for so long, has cracked under the weight of wet leaves and sunk to earth adding a new mass on the ground. Each drop of rain tells a story, each drip and splatter marks a place with sounds which create an aural reality for the lives of others.

Autumn begins to glow with the first breaks of sunlight. The apple crop is heavy. Blackberries ripen early. Hips and haws are bursting with scarlet and deep red vitamins of exuberance. Gentle days they may be but

Dove Plantation, Easthope

everything turns to food and appetites, like the edge to the air, are keen. Even the trees are sucking goodness from their leaves before they turn and fall. The first of the ivy flowers are opening, busy with flies and bees cramming as much nectar as they can get. This is the time for feeding up because none of us know what's around the corner.

Charms of chaffinch and goldfinch move between a tall lime tree and electricity cables strung across a field. They perch on the wires, little black dots on lines like the musical score of their own rapid twitterings. There are slots in the clayey earth between a few pale-blue flowers of speedwell, prints clear and pointed cross the field towards the woods where fallow deer have run this morning. From a stile at wood's edge the view is sudden and dramatic over the foxy pelt of oak woods to the Wrekin.

There is a low layer of purple-grey cloud, but underneath and above it the sky is as blue as the speedwell flowers. A beam of bright sunlight scans along hills rising from the Shropshire Plain, making them look more like dune systems than wooded hills. In the distance, a grey plume rises from the chipboard factory in Chirk across the Welsh border; it stands against the dark wall of hills which roll into the high Berwyns beyond. The long sweep of Wenlock Edge curves away to the southwest and its woods, mottled with browns and yellows are still. Cutting across this unusually farseeing light, following the hedge line along the wood, a peacock butterfly, seen only as a black fragment, flies into those fleeting moments only detected in the corner of the eye.

The hawk lands in a small tree. It settles on a branch only four feet off the ground and arranges its wings, shrugging shoulders under a dark overcoat. Its chest is pale, drizzled with fawns and browns and yellow legs end in talons which nail into the bark. The sparrowhawk keeps very still, but for its head which switches from side to side, so its eyes can watch the traffic of low autumn sunlight through the jiggling bluster of leaves.

Harton Hollow Wood

A breeze shoves stiffly, twisting the leaves, shining on one side, glancing off the other, as their stalks strain against branches to follow the autumnal migration into the earth. Ash leaves, last to come, first to go, are turning lime-green and falling. Linden trees and hazel are showing yellow ochre; elder burns red from the bottom up. The sparrowhawk remains still, watching the forensic details of a small world get smaller: pinpoints of white holly flowers in their glossy darkness, speckled wood and small tortoiseshell butterflies, moths over bending grass stems, shadows which belong to nothing.

There are other raptors in the sky; bigger, blunter, more powerful. Buzzards are sliding along the breeze, tacking through long loops of air, turning slowly with one wing pressed against an invisible column. They are dark and heavy with the light behind them, but when it spills under their wings they are pale, bronze and tawny. It is the autumn equinox, a kind of balance of day and night in a year whose seasons have slewed a bit. But this feels right; the buzzards turning silently through the wind, leaves spiralling to the ground, kinds of balance within kinds of light.

Small birds avoid the place where the sparrowhawk sits in the tree. It has ducked out of the wind to watch the world move at its own pace, without a hawk's blurring speed. But that is about to change. The hawk turns on the branch, and in one movement as its wings and tail-feathers open, it spins away through the branches.

Under a high blue sky in dazzling light, the oak trees reach the peak of their autumn colour. This is not as bright as the buttercup-yellow of field maples, the brimstone of larches, the brassy flakes of birch or the burnished copper of beeches. It is a smouldering fire that has taken weeks to ignite the canopies of leaves,

now it's glowing through the spectrum of gold all across the landscape in every direction. Although each oak, apart from the odd exception, does not burn as brightly as other trees, collectively they look astonishing.

In a land of woods, copses, hedgerows and open-grown individual trees, the oaks assert a presence more powerfully than all the others. There is something about this presence which suddenly redefines the landscape. This is not so much in the sense of a hierarchy of values amongst the trees, although it's easy to see why the oak has such an iconic status in lowland Britain, but more as a signifier of place. Here is a landscape whose natural and cultural histories have melded into one visual substance, a moment when the old tensions between countryside and wild Nature seem to balance out. But this is just a flare. It is a matter of hours before the winds and heavy rains come back, tearing through the trees, flooding off the fields.

When the weather swings round to dive down from the northeast, it brings the migrant thrushes. They come in the cold clear nights guided by stars from Scandinavia, Finland, Siberia and Iceland. Now the air is full of redwings and fieldfares, the blackbirds which follow them and even a band of siskins. A flock of about 200 redwings passes over Windmill Hill to raid the woods for berries. Fieldfares have stripped a big old yew tree and move methodically through hedges. The last couple of autumns have seen rich harvests of fruits and berries which seems to have contributed to the breeding success of winter migrants from the north.

Like the ace of spades, a Lime leaf hangs on a spider's web from the hedge. Lemon on one side, ochre on the other, the leaf rotates one way, then back, slowly reflecting low autumn sunlight. A wind blowing across

ferny banks of limes and oaks. Under a stand of wild service trees, whose leaves have turned deep orange, a fallow deer walks, sniffing the air and watching. Above her the morning moon hangs halfway in the sky, as if suspended like the ace of spades leaf from gossamer. Whatever destiny holds for any of us here, the same wind blows through it, the same light shines, the same white smudge of cloud shrouds in mystery.

Outside the wood, a breeze is beginning to spin the flash of copper-yellow off beech and lime trees. Soon the breeze is shunted by a southwesterly wind onto the canopy to roll and roar up Wenlock Edge along the steep brow of trees which follows its flow instead of damming the wave. Inside the wood it is cooler, stiller, greener. A light rain has made the clay sticky under foot and the air is damp and studied through the trees. It is early yet. The sun has not had time to break into the grey which binds the colours together, but it is coming. From under the wind, on the path above Lea Quarry looking towards Brown Clee to the southeast, trees cast long shadows across a swell of fields: some tawny with combine lines and bale stacks, some green and white-dotted with sheep. Down in the quarry, pudding heaps of grey grit pile around the turquoise lake and pale limestone walls.

the field has got the horses going and the six of them suddenly take off, all thudding hooves and streaming manes, running through bright air with blowing leaves. A gang of rooks and jackdaws mobs four buzzards above the trees. The birds clatter, the horses gallop, the leaves blow and the ace of spades twists on its thread showing its two faces of luck.

Nearby, late blooms of nettle-leaved bellflower are a much deeper purple-blue than they were in summer. Following my steps is what sounds like a bicycle of leaves. Pheasants crouch in corduroy fields as shotguns pop and bang across the valley. On the threshold of the woods, a small group of fallow deer know bad luck smells human and they run into the shadows stirring leaves. There, the top of an oak has fallen, breaking branches of one of the ancient lime pollards. These venerable hollow trees are sentinels, watching over the steep

A small flock of around 16 Hebridean sheep; small, neat, horned and raven-black, graze on wiry grass and wild flowers at the quarry's lip. These are very different animals to the white woolly dots in the distance; smaller, edgily wary, feral, dignified in their Celtic horns and completely the opposite colour. As if to endorse this, a raven scoots across the wind to drop into the quarry. It dances, back-flips, stoops and soars. As the sun brightens, colours emerge: scarlet hips, pink spindle berries, purple-brown hawthorn leaves and the beech-copper and black script of an opening comma butterfly's wings. In these days around an autumn full moon, the season has a fiery taste.

Buzzards fly into a pale blue sky, sketched high with vapour trails and cirrus cloud. They cruise on a warm thermal, a church steeple-high orbit that draws circling lines, looping over back gardens, the priory ruins and surrounding fields. Two buzzards spar playfully as they rise higher and a third joins them. The pale undersides of their wings flash silver in the sun and their catlike calls are soft, stringing out into a space of warm autumn light. As they ascend the three are joined by a fourth, then the four are joined by a fifth. Five buzzards, weaving pentagram patterns higher in the sky, become black specks as they drift northwest, out of Wenlock's hollow, over the Edge to the plain and Severn Vale beyond. It's as if the history of a moment is being written by these birds as they soar above other histories which are equally ephemeral.

A hundred feet above Harley Bank, recent works to stabilise the rock where the road cuts up the wooded Edge has left raw scars and a new path and fence. From the highest point, the view follows the buzzard's pathway through the sky, above the plain to the far hills. The midnight harvests, where combines worked day and night while the weather held, are in and the earth is being turned and seeded again. The last colours bleed from woods and hedges; yellows and ochres in lime and ash and the red splash of field maple. A haze veils the uncertain world beyond. But this is a certain place, a high exposed point which takes in the miles of landscape like a buzzard's eye; a place from which to ambush the thoughts of travellers in the cutting far below. The view from Edge Top, in the corner of a field called Gallows-Tree Leasowe, is the last thing many would see, hanging from a rope.

Fungi

by John Hughes

Way back, when you were at school you probably took a subject called biology. *Bi* (two) *ology* (science); the study of the two kingdoms of nature, plants and animals. Fungi were classified as 'lower plants'. Our understanding of evolution has, well, evolved and, while there is on-going debate, it is generally reckoned that there are seven kingdoms in nature. Of these seven, four comprise simple creatures such as types of bacteria and blue-green algae, but plants, animals and fungi are all kingdoms in their own right.

It's not surprising that fungi were regarded as plants. They tend to grow in the same place and can't move around in the way that animals can. However, their lack of chlorophyll to manufacture their own food makes them closer to animals. They also contain a chemical called chitin, which is the protein that makes up the shells of insects; decomposing fungi distinctly smell of rotting meat rather than vegetables.

Misunderstood, or what?

Today, there's a growing concern that children don't know where milk comes from, can't name basic vegetables and are unable to identify the song of a Blackbird. However, even the most erudite country person seems to struggle with fungi.

"They'll kill the trees"

"Don't touch them they're poisonous"

"If they peel you can eat 'em"

Mushroom myths abound, so before talking about what's on Wenlock Edge let me try to demystify them a little.

How do fungi work?

With fungi, what you see is decidedly *not* what you get. The mushrooms and toadstools that pop up in the woodlands of the Edge in autumn are but a tiny proportion of a fraction of the tip of the iceberg. Everywhere, under the ground, in the leaf litter, in dead wood and inside living trees, there are microscopic white threads called hyphae that permeate anywhere there might be food. Hyphae mass together to form the thin, but visible threads called mycelia that are the vegetative 'body' of the fungus.

Food for a fungus is likely to be almost anything that has died. Just like animals, different fungi specialise

in consuming different things. Unlike animals, fungi digest their food outside their 'bodies' with the fungal threads being supremely efficient at absorbing available nutrients.

Nature's recyclers

Carbon and nitrogen are locked up in all living things and need to be cycled and recycled. Fungi play an essential role in this. Take the humble cow pat. This is semi-digested herbage and an ideal source of food. Insects are the most obvious cow pat visitors on a warm summer day, but fungi will be there too.

Most likely, the cow will have eaten spores and you can follow a fascinating sequence of fungi 'flowering', if you bother to get up close and personal with the

pat. Each species of fungus will specialise and rapidly run through its life cycle making way for the next species. The first will tackle the tough cellulose, softening it up for the next and the next until the carbon, nitrogen and trace elements are returned to the soil to be taken up by plants. A system where nothing is wasted and everything is used an infinite number of times.

Reproduction

The reproduction of fungi is very complex. Most will reproduce vegetatively (bits breaking off and continuing to grow), asexually (producing 'clones') and sexually. It is sexual reproduction that gives rise to mushrooms and toadstools, which are nothing more than fruit.

Technically, a mushroom is a 'fruiting body', but think of it more as a seed pod. A typical mushroom contains a mind-blowing number of seeds. Fungal seeds are known as spores and they are microscopically small. This enables the fungus to produce them by the billion. The 100mm cap of an average mushroom may well release 16 billion (that's 16,000,000,000) spores.

Structure

The structure of a typical mushroom is a stalk holding up a cap, under which are gills. Gills are folds of flesh that create a huge surface area, enough to hold 16 billion spores in fact. Fungi have really strong geotropism and will always try to turn to the horizontal. The spores then fall cleanly from the gills and be caught by wind currents to be dispersed. The stem raises the cap a few centimetres to where the air is turbulent to ensure spores are carried away from the parent.

Most spores will land no more than a few metres away, after all that's likely to be suitable habitat. But spores can be carried for miles; indeed they can make their way into the upper atmosphere and circumnavigate the globe. Most will perish, but with such vast numbers if a tiny percentage survive and grow, then the fungus will flourish. In this way fungi have been able to colonise virtually every habitat on the planet.

Fairy rings

So, assume a spore lands somewhere it is able to grow. It germinates and sends out white threads in every direction. If it finds food this will continue. Thus the shape described by the fungus is a circle that is growing larger and larger, like a ripple on a pond. Food and warmth will stimulate growth, which in turn encourages reproduction at the outer edge of the circle.

Consequently, when climatic conditions are favourable, a ring of mushrooms will appear, a fairy ring. Each year this ring will grow larger, typically increasing its diameter by 150mm. In this way it's possible to measure the ring and estimate its age. Rings of Cloud Cap *Clitocybe nebularis* are a common sight on the Edge, but on these steep, wooded slopes rings become indistinct and hidden amongst the brambles.

Who's the daddy?

Until recent times it was impossible to determine the size of a large woodland ring. How was it possible to work out whether the fruit bodies were heralding from one or more individual organisms? Technology, in the form of genetic fingerprinting, means that this is now possible.

In the vast tracts of virgin forest in America just such a study was undertaken. A type of honey fungus was found to have individuals that stretched over 50km. Logically this means that fungi are the daddy of all living things; being bigger older and heavier that any other creature, *probably!* 'Probably' because it's impossible to prove. You can't dig up and weigh all the mycelial threads; you can't carbon date it because individual threads are short-lived and constantly being re-grown.

A question for Darwin

Like all life on Earth, fungi have adapted and evolved to exploit a niche. New species have evolved; in Britain alone there are thought to be about 4500 larger fungi (that produce visible mushrooms and toadstools) and a similar number of microfungi (yeasts and moulds). Compare this with the paltry 1500 species of flowering plants we have!

When Darwin examined the beaks of island races of finches on the Galapagos he reasoned that their shape had evolved to suit their habitat needs. Short, strong beaks for breaking seeds and long, slender beaks for probing flowers for nectar.

What would Darwin have made of fungi? There is astonishing variety in size, shape and colour of fruiting bodies. They contain a bewildering array of chemicals that give them smell and taste, or that are toxic to other species. Some even glow in the dark. Now remember that these are all seed pods, mostly dropping spores into the air for a week or two. They generally do not need to attract or repel animals. So Mr Darwin, what is the evolutionary advantage to the diversity of appearance of fungi? If Darwin didn't answer this please don't expect me to.

Fungi are there as testament to the complexity, ingenuity and brilliance of nature. They should also remind us to exercise a little humility. We may think we have an encyclopaedic knowledge of nature, but there is still lots to learn and, as we destroy species after species with our thoughtless greed, just what are we losing? One thing is for certain, without fungi our species is doomed.

Fungi and trees

Fossils

Wenlock Edge stands out as a landscape feature because of its trees. And where there are trees you will find fungi, but why? Fungi and trees have evolved together over millions of years, so much so that one certainly fails to thrive without the other. You would not think that fungi fossilise terribly well, but fossils of early land plants from 400 million years ago show evidence of microscopic fungal features showing that a close relationship already existed between the two kingdoms.

We've already explored the notion of fungi as nature's recyclers, making food available to plants that would otherwise be locked up in wood, leaves, dead animals and dung. An examination of fallen branches or log piles along the Edge will reveal fungi rotting and recycling throughout the year.

Rotters

A striking and common example of a recycler is the Yellow Staghorn Fungus *Calocera viscosa* often to be found on decaying stumps. Its vivid yellow-orange colour stands out against the dark green mosses that it is frequently found with. Less conspicuous, but well worth looking for are the small black and white fingers of the Candle Snuff Fungus *Xylaria hypoxylon*, looking for the world like the wick of a candle that has just been blown out. The small size of these fruit bodies belies the power of their mycelia to feast on wood and return it to the soil.

Rotting fungi can also be found on living trees. But remember that wood at the heart of a tree is no longer alive. From mid summer look out for the neon yellow brackets of Chicken of the Woods *Laetoporus sulphureaus* growing out of Ash, Oak and Beech trees. This fungus will decompose the heartwood, but that doesn't mean the tree is doomed. Hollow trees are commonplace in natural woodlands. In fact there is good evidence from the 1987 'hurricane' that hollow trees are more wind firm than solid ones.

Ash trees are everywhere on the Edge and any fallen branch can reward you with the black excrescences of King Alfred's Cakes *Daldinia concentrica*. These cling tenaciously to the wood, but prise one off and it will reveal its internal structure of concentric rings that give it its scientific name. Once removed, don't discard it as it makes a superb fire-lighting tinder and it is said to cure cramp.

Kind killers

Fungi kill trees, that's a fact. Everyone knows the reputation of Honey Fungus *Armillaria spp.* It appears on Wenlock Edge (as it does in all other woods) in early October in large clumps on the ground and on trees. But if it's in all the woods, how come there are still living trees? Similarly, Birch Polypore *Piptoporus betulinus* will be there wherever there are birch trees. Standing dead and fallen birch logs sprout this bracket, also known as the Razor Strop Fungus because it can be used to sharpen cutthroat razors.

If it was in the interest of fungi to kill off trees they could have achieved it with ease over the last 400 million years. Quite the reverse is true. It is clearly in the interest of fungi that trees thrive so they have food and a home. Fungi that kill trees are doing so to keep the population of trees healthy.

No one quite understands the mechanism, but it appears that potentially pathogenic fungi, like Birch Polypore, live benignly in trees for most, if not all of their lives. When a tree becomes stressed through drought, damage or disease the fungus alters its behaviour and kills the tree. As the tree falls it opens up the woodland canopy, making way for saplings to thrive, thus maintaining a healthy tree population of diverse age. Killing an individual Birch tree is bizarrely an act of kindness to the species *Betula pendula*.

Best mates

The third tree-fungus relationship is the most profound. Known as a mycorrhizal association, this is true symbiosis with both parties receiving very significant benefit. Mycorrhizal fungi can be found growing on, in and around the roots of host trees. Fungi are exceptional at absorbing soil nutrients, which they share with the

tree. Trees excel at producing their own food from photosynthesis and share these sugars with the fungus. That's a real win-win.

Only some fungi are mycorrhizal and some of those will only form a relationship with certain trees. Find a red and white spotted Fly Agaric *Amanita muscaria* and while you may not see a pixie sitting on it, you almost certainly will see a Birch tree close by.

Some trees seem to have numerous mycorrhizal associations, notable here are Oak, Birch and Beech making them a must to investigate when on a fungal foray. Some though have few associations, Ash being the most obvious example along the Edge. Because Ash is a (if not the) dominant tree on the limey soil, it can make the Edge woodlands disappointing for fungi.

Sycamore too tends to have a dearth of fungi. Naturalists continue to argue whether this maple is native or introduced. In the past, its lack of associated fungi has been used as an argument that it is non-native. Modern thinking is that mycorrhizal fungi are so important to the health of trees they may well occur in their seeds.

Without its clothing of trees, Wenlock Edge would look very different, but its trees need the fungi that kill, cure and cosset them. This ancient alliance keeps the woodlands healthy and in good heart.

Orchids and other lime lovers

Trees aren't the only plants where there is a mycorrhizal association. The shallow lime-rich soils of the Edge have a wealth of wildflowers because there are few nutrients, which suppresses many of the more aggressive plants. Many of the wildflowers will have a fungal association, but orchids rely on it perhaps even more than trees.

Orchid seed is like dust, too small to carry any significant food reserve making germination tricky. Mycorrhizal fungi are essential to kick-start the growth of many orchids and to ensure they find sufficient nutrients when they become mature plants.

Fungi of the fields

The limestone grasslands of Wenlock Edge abound with flowers in the spring and summer. But in some years this colourful extravaganza continues into the autumn. Fungi are as plentiful in the fields as in the woods. Different species find a niche feeding on the dead vegetation. Many are small, brown and insignificant, while still crucial to maintaining nature's balance.

The shining stars of grassland fungi have to be the waxcaps *Hygrocybe spp.* Often modest in size, waxcaps shine out like a treasure chest of jewels: red, yellow, orange, green, white, pink, black. In occasional years they are in such profusion they can make the wildflowers seem drab.

Keep it short

Because they don't photosynthesise, there is a misconception that fungi don't need light. Light is essential to successful fruiting. In autumn, look in a field of long grass and you'll find very few fungi. If the same field is mown short or grazed there are likely to be many more fruiting bodies. Light penetrating the ground stimulates fruiting.

This makes perfect sense. In the long grass it would be difficult for a small fungus to successfully disperse its spores over a reasonable distance; the grasses would act as a barrier and slow the wind.

One of the problems with Wenlock Edge grasslands has been that grazing has been limited, largely because

fields are too small or inaccessible. When nibbling sheep or a mower is reintroduced, the flowers will thrive and the waxcaps soon make a comeback. Fungi seem to be very resilient, living on happily in the soil biding their time until conditions are just right for fruiting.

Edible and poisonous

It's very anthropocentric to think that fungi can be classified as edible and poisonous to humans. And it's down right foolish to believe that there would be simple method of distinguishing the two types. Their role in maintaining the delicate balance of life on Earth is neither to feed nor to poison *Homo sapiens*.

Good, bad and... indifferent
The reality is that there will be hundreds of species of fungi to be found on Wenlock Edge. Of those, a handful, perhaps twenty, are good to eat and a similar number hold the potential to kill you. In between is every imaginable shade of grey. The vast majority won't harm you, but they won't taste very good either.

I'm a fan of picking for the pot and I would encourage anyone beginning to become interested in fungi to follow suit. Fungi are a difficult subject to break into. There are thousands of species, many looking very similar. Limiting yourself to identifying a few edible species (and the ones you might confuse them for, of course) is a manageable task that you can build on with each new mushrooming year.

Good eating
So, taking an autumn stroll through the Wenlock woods what might you find worth collecting for dinner? Let's start with a guaranteed find every year, Honey Fungus *Armillaria spp.* Collect Honey Fungus when it's at the button mushroom stage and it is truly delicious. One note of caution, don't be tempted to eat it raw. It contains a mild toxin that is destroyed by the heat of cooking. This toxin makes it taste soapy.

Wood Blewits *Lepista nuda* are another assured find, usually from late October. Blue is the colour, eating is the game, the cap, the gills and the stem are all suffused with a beautiful blue colour that fades brown with age. Blewits have a delicate perfumed smell that comes

through in their flavour. It has a close cousin, the Field Blewit *Lepista saeva* which looks similar, but grows in grasslands, has a vivid violet stem and makes equally good eating.

You should certainly expect to find Field Mushrooms *Agaricus campestris* but this is just one of 30-odd species of true mushrooms *Agaricus* and, for me, a better find would be Horse Mushroom *A. arvensis*. This is larger, sometimes dinner plate-sized, has a subtle aroma of aniseed and will bruise faintly yellow. If your mushroom immediately bruises bright yellow then beware, you have probably picked a Yellow Stainer *A. xanthodermus* that may cause you severe gastric upset.

Not all fungi have gills. Look under the cap and sometimes you'll find a different structure creating large surface area for spore production. One such is the Hedgehog Mushroom *Hydnum repandum*, this has soft spines that easily break off. This has the dual advantage of being difficult to confuse with other species and has a delicious nutty flavour. An added bonus is that it never suffers from wriggling maggots.

Perhaps the greatest edible reward is also one without

gills. It appears to have a 'sponge' (in fact a number of tubes) under the cap. The Penny Bun or cep *Boletus edulis* is prized throughout Europe and can regularly be found along Wenlock Edge. These mushroom live up to their Italian name of 'Porcini' (little pigs) as they are plump and meaty with the finest flavour of all wild mushrooms. Remember, not all mushrooms with tubes are ceps. There are many *Boletus* species, very few of which are harmful.

Truffles

I can't talk about Wenlock Edge's edible fungi without mentioning truffles. Now I've never actually found truffles along the Edge, but I am sure they are there. This may come as a surprise if you think truffles are merely an exotic import from France and Italy. The UK has over 20 species of true truffles *Tuber spp.* but the only one to have any economic value is the Summer Truffle *T. aestivum*.

Truffles are associated with a number of trees (notably Oak, Beech and Hazel) and thrive on limestone. Summer Truffle has been recorded on Benthall Edge, (the northern extremity of Wenlock Edge) by Sir Paul Benthall of Benthall Hall in the mid 20th century. Unlike other fungal fruit bodies, truffles are completely subterranean and can only be found through opportunistic digging or a trained dog.

Being buried, truffles rely on their strong smell to attract insects, molluscs and mammals which eat them and disperse their spore via their dung. It is this smell and taste that makes them so highly prized. Summer Truffle sells for around £10 per 25g (1oz). Sadly your chances of making a fortune from Wenlock truffles are slim, but it's still worth looking for them.

Steps to finding a truffle:

- Choose a sunny September day to go for a walk on Wenlock Edge
- Select a mature Beech tree with little or no vegetation underneath it
- Get on your knees about 2m from the tree trunk
- Get out your trusty truffle rake (a stick is a poor man's alternative)
- Carefully rake away the fallen leaves and decomposing leaf litter
- Have ready a basket and a witty response should a party of ramblers pass by
- Summer truffles are spherical, black and warty and will be anywhere from on the surface to 100mm under the ground
- Carefully place all your truffles in a basket, weigh them and decide how many to sell and how many to keep
- Replace all the raked up leaves

I strongly suspect that I am one of the very few people who has searched for truffles on Wenlock Edge. I know I was only a few metres away from finding one. With your help we will find a glut next year.

Poison

It's probably easier to find a fungal feast than to poison yourself on Wenlock Edge. That said, there are a number growing there best avoided. An easy mistake to make is to confuse the parasol mushrooms. Excellent eating is the Parasol Mushroom *Macrolepiota procera* with its snake skin-patterned stem. However, the Shaggy Parasol *M. rhacodes* can make you ill. To paraphrase a friend who accidentally ate one "I had the runs for three days!" To distinguish them, bruise the base of the stem...if it turns bright orange leave well alone.

Often camouflaged by its drab greeny-brown colour is the Ugly Milkcap *Lactarius turpis*. Like all milkcaps it exudes a milky sap when the flesh is broken. A tiny drop of milk on the tip or your tongue will be sufficient to tell you it tastes hot, very hot. If you were able to swallow a chunk of this mushroom its irritant milk would cause it to come back up again pretty quickly.

Don't expect wasp-like warning colours to alert you to toxic toadstools. In some years the White Fibrecap *Inocybe geophylla* will be in profusion along tracks and in hedge bottoms together with a lilac coloured variety. These are no more than 50mm tall, but like other fibrecaps can be deadly.

Death cap

The mushroom responsible for the majority of poisonings throughout Europe can occasionally be found all along Wenlock Edge. The aptly named Death Cap *Amanita phalloides* has a most attractive green-grey cap and stands about 150mm tall. It has pure white gills and, at the base of the stem, is the remains of a fleshy sack that enclosed and protected the fruit body before it emerged; these are features typical of Amanita and should set alarm bells ringing for anyone collecting for the pot.

Consuming around half a cap will be sufficient to kill an adult. Cooking, freezing and drying does not diminish its toxicity, but only about 50% of people eating death cap are killed by it. But don't take this to mean that your chances of survival are evens. The toxins attack and degenerate your liver and kidneys meaning that you will be severely disabled should you survive.

Finding, identifying and understanding fungi

I am confident that by now you are confused and terrified at the thought of collecting and identifying, let alone eating fungi. Please don't be. The trick is to start in a small way and build up your knowledge. A good identification guide is a must (I like Roger Phillips' *'Mushrooms'*) but illustrations of hundreds of species will leave you bewildered. I have two suggestions as a way to ease you into this tricky discipline.

Start in the spring

In late April and May there is a small flush of mushrooms, far fewer than in autumn. This makes them simpler to identify. You are almost bound to find the pure white St George's Mushroom *Tricholoma gambosum* growing in rings around the woodland edge. This is a good eater if you can beat the maggots (or you're not squeamish). Bizarre-looking conical and convoluted morels *Morchella spp.* appear in the woodlands every few years, especially around old bonfire sites. More good eating.

Cup fungi are a spring speciality. The olive-brown Bay Cup *Peziza badia* grows flush to the ground, often on sawdust or buried wood. Throughout late winter and early spring the Scarlet Elf Cup *Sarcoscypha coccinea* brighten up the woodland floor before it is clothed by spring flowers.

Fungus forays

In autumn be on the look out for organised fungus forays. Groups such as National Trust and Shropshire Wildlife Trust put on these events, led by an expert who will give you tips to get you going. Be modest; make it your ambition to learn five new species each year and by year three you'll qualify as an expert!

Truly understanding fungi will take a little longer. Walking a stretch of woodland regularly enables you to build up a picture of what grows where. Trust me, you'll remember where the edible ones grow.

Finding striking–looking fungi is always memorable. One of the specialities of the Edge are Earth Stars *Geastrum triplex*. These are puffballs contained within fleshy sacks that burst open and curl back on themselves to raise the spore sack off the ground. Their structure is as fascinating as it is beautiful. Equally fascinating is the Stinkhorn *Phallus impudicus*. Its shape is distinctly, um, phallic and it smells of rotting meat or worse. Its spores are a slimy mass on the top of the stem and are dispersed by flies attracted to the foetid smell.

It's not really necessary to be able to identify or indeed know anything about the astonishing part played by fungi in nature to appreciate them. They are an amazing area of wildlife that bring pleasure and interest to a walk in the countryside. But a little awareness and understanding helps us all to value the variety of life and its habitats.

Conserving the fungi of Wenlock Edge

National Trust has been acquiring chunks of Wenlock Edge so it can be conserved for everyone to enjoy. Plans are drawn up and teams of contractors and volunteers undertake management work to conserve those elements deemed precious.

It should come as no surprise that I'm all for conserving fungi. The problem is how? To understand whether management has been successful there is a series of simple steps:
* Survey what's there
* Work out what you want and how to get it
* Carry out management
* Monitor any changes

The difficulty with fungi is that they are fickle. You only know if they're present when they fruit. A few types fruit every year without fail, but many will go five, ten, twenty years between fruiting. They will only fruit following a very specific set of climatic conditions and in a time of climate change who knows what this will do to fungi?

It is a lifetime's job just to build up a picture of what grows on any particular site. Then the capriciousness of fungi makes working out what you want and how to get it the work of another lifetime.

So, when considering the conservation of fungi we have to adopt a somewhat different approach. It is anyway good nature conservation practice not to become too fixated on any one group or species. Much better is to think more broadly about the habitat. If the habitat is healthy species diversity will follow.

With this in mind it is possible to set out some basic principles that will allow fungi to thrive:

Don't be tidy minded. Fallen trees and branches look untidy to some people and need to be sawn up and taken away. These are food for fungus and ultimately food for the next generation of trees.

Grow old gracefully. An ancient hollow tree is not a species, it's a habitat in its own right. These forest veterans often have a unique array of species of fungi and insects associated with them. Allow some trees

to become hollow giants and make sure there is a new generation of veterans ready when the ancient ones finally fall.

Stick to natives, mostly. Native trees that is, but first decide which ones are truly native. Ash should probably be the dominant tree of Wenlock Edge, but this would reduce its fungal diversity. There is a place for trees such as Beech, Sycamore and Larch that have been introduced and are well established.

All ages welcome. Maintain a diverse age structure to the woodlands. Active management helps this process and creates short-term niches such as glades that will be exploited by many creatures.

Graze the grasslands. Species-rich limestone grasslands are a rare resource and need nurturing. Wildflowers and fungi will only thrive with appropriate grazing. It is a joy to see National Trust Hebridean sheep knocking the grasslands around Lea Quarry into shape.

Why bother?

I hope this chapter has spelt out why we should all care about the fungi of Wenlock Edge. Fungi are easily forgotten as they are largely hidden and poorly understood. But without their fungi the woodlands of the Edge would look very different and perhaps not exist at all. Woodlands are far more than trees. They are one of the richest terrestrial habitats we have. Slugs, snails and insects (all the creatures we also forget about) rely on mushrooms as a source of food to see them through the winter. But above all, fungi are part of the diversity of the ecosystem and diversity means balance. It is a balanced and healthy Wenlock Edge we all want to bequeath to future generations.

Eaton Coppice

Woodlands
then & now

by Ray Hawes

We can be certain that although trees may have dominated this area for a very long time, the species and character of tree cover will have changed many times over the years; the woodland we have today has never been on the Edge before and will not return again. What are the influences that have driven these changes over the years, what type of woodland exists today and how is this likely to change in the future?

Introduction

The dominant visual impact of Wenlock Edge is created by the vegetation. The woodland defines and outlines the geology and land-use of Wenlock Edge, clinging to the escarpment face and remaining on the steepest slopes where agricultural improvement has not been possible.

The majority of Wenlock Edge is classified as an Ancient Woodland Site. This means that it has had woodland cover since at least 1600AD, we can be pretty certain that there have been trees here for much longer than that. It is possible that, because of its particular characteristics, the Edge has been

virtually continuously wooded since trees returned to the British Isles following the ending of the last ice age around 10,000 years ago. There would have also have been trees and tree-like vegetation here many millions of years before the last ice age; apart from the odd possible fossil record we do not know much about these times. There is therefore no ecological continuity or link back to vegetation before the last ice age.

Following the Ice Age

Wenlock Edge, along with the majority of the British Isle, was covered in ice during the last glacial period which started some 110,000 years ago and reached its maximum extent around 20,000 years ago. This 'last ice age' as it is commonly (incorrectly) described, receded north about 10,000 years ago (8,000BC) and as it did the land left uncovered by the melting ice began to revegetate. Unsurprisingly there are no actual records of the species and type of flora which colonised the virtually bare ground, however pollen studies have enabled the spread of tree species to be mapped. The natural reintroduction of trees was through the land connection to the European continent in the south east of England, although Hazel seems to have recolonised from around the Irish Sea i.e. the west, oak coming from a refuge area to the south and west of Cornwall. The rising sea levels caused by the melting ice inundated the south-western refuge and removed the land connection to what we now know as France between 5 and 8,000 years ago, limiting natural recolonisation. There was therefore only a maximum of around 5,000 years for this process to take place, accounting for the relatively few tree species that are generally accepted to be truly native here, compared with our continental neighbours.

Tree species that are thought to have arrived naturally by 7,000 years ago in the area we now know as Shropshire would have included: Juniper, Downy and Silver Birch, Aspen, various willows, Scots Pine, Common Alder, Hazel, Small Leaved Lime, Bird Cherry, Wych Elm, Rowan, Sessile and Pedunculate Oak, Holly, Hawthorn and Yew. They would not have all arrived at the same time and may not have all found their way to Wenlock Edge, even if they did conditions may not have been suitable for some of them.

The 'wildwood', which developed through the recolonisation process would have been very variable across the British Isles, its species and structure dependant mainly on the geology, soil characteristics, topography and aspect of where it was growing. At its most dominant the wildwood covered around 85% of the land with only the highest mountains and some coastal and very wet areas remaining treeless. The 'wood' on Wenlock Edge would therefore only have been a small part of virtually continuous tree cover across most of England and Wales.

There has been much debate amongst woodland specialists over the years about the character of the wildwood; some suggesting that it would have been very dense, almost unbroken woodland, others arguing that there would have been much open space, more like what we would now call wood pasture. It is most likely that the wildwood actually consisted of extensive tracts of dense woodland, areas with no trees and everything in between. These areas would not have remained the same; there would have been constant changes over time because of natural events such as storms and the effects of grazing animals.

The first 'woodland' on Wenlock Edge

Tree cover on the slopes of Wenlock Edge would have developed differently to the areas around because of the unique geology and steepness. Soils would have developed more slowly and would have been much more base-rich than those off the Edge, due to the underlying limestone rocks and the tendency of soil to 'creep' down hills. Woody vegetation would therefore have started colonising by taking advantage of less steep areas where soil could accumulate. Tree cover

would have consequently been quite patchy, the species that would particularly have been able to establish, survive and eventually thrive in these conditions include Hazel, Elm, Small and Large Leaved Lime and probably later Ash. Whilst oak and other species such as Alder and Birch may have found some areas suitable for their requirements, it is unlikely they would have been on the steeper slopes in any great numbers in the early days. As vegetation cover developed, soil condition and depth would have increased allowing better tree growth, allowing other species opportunities to establish.

Over the next couple of thousand years, other tree species such as Whitebeam, Ash, Large-leaved Lime, Wild Cherry, Field Maple and Wild Service Tree would have arrived. Within dense woodlands, tree species that could survive in low light levels such as Lime, Wych Elm, Holly and Yew would dominate, whereas species such as Ash, Oak and Cherry which need full overhead light to thrive depended on open areas to increase their numbers. Over long periods of time, species would vary in location and abundance, with the colonisation of open areas by short lived pioneer species being replaced by longer-lived trees, before climatic events such as storms, droughts and possibly fires created gaps for the process to begin again. At this time, Mesolithic man's influence would have been minor but the indigenous large herbivores such as Red Deer, Elk, Boar and Aurochs, the original wild cattle, would have affected the makeup of woods to some extent, probably on a very local level.

Man begins to make a difference

Having been left relatively untouched to develop naturally for around 4,000 years, man started to have a significant effect on the wildwood from the start of

the Neolithic Age, around 3,800BC. The population of the UK increased rapidly through immigration; cleared agricultural land was required for their cereal crops and domestic animals. Polished stone axes were used to clear the woods and to manage them by coppicing and pollarding, the produce being used for building, fencing and animal fodder. Pollen analysis identifies a rapid decrease in the amount of Elm present over the British Isles, this could be attributed to woodland clearance, the use of Elm for animal fodder and possibly an early occurrence of Dutch Elm Disease. Although it is unlikely that the trees on Wenlock Edge would have been substantially cleared for agricultural use, as there were other flatter and easier areas, it could have provided woody products for nearby communities.

Although the absence of easily-available water sources near the Edge would also have restricted settlements, coppice products would have been put to many uses including constructing shelters. The faster growing the poles, the more pliable they were; Hazel would have been particularly valuable, as the products of coppicing had many uses and the nuts provided an important food source. Whilst larger trees were normally of less worth because of the effort required to fell and reduce them to manageable sizes, the regrowth from the cut stumps was much more use. This could be considered as the first form of woodland management! It is also probable that pollarding was 'discovered' at this time, the greater effort required to cut the tree at head height being rewarded with regrowth that was out of the reach of browsing animals.

As the Neolithic moved into the Bronze- and then Iron ages, the population continued to increase and the tools needed to clear woodland for agriculture and manage coppice etc. became more efficient. The woodlands

around Wenlock Edge would have been progressively cleared but tree cover on the Edge itself would have remained largely intact. Larger settlements would still have been located near to rivers and areas of lighter soils where tilling would be easier, so at the end of the Iron Age the tree cover on the Edge would not have been greatly altered.

What the Romans did and how the Anglo–Saxons carried on up to 1066

During Roman times, the rate of woodland clearance continued as it had done towards the end of the Iron Age; this was the most active period of wildwood destruction in history. It is thought that in the seven hundred year period, 300BC until 400AD, half of the land area in the lowland part of England was cleared of woodland. The growing population required larger areas dedicated to food production, so more difficult areas to farm had to be cleared and used. The products from woodlands were essential to maintain necessary industries and to make life more pleasurable. For example, large quantities of fuelwood were required for iron smelting, it has been estimated that 84 tons of wood were needed to produce the charcoal to make one ton of iron. More wood was also required for making bricks and tiles, for building in general and for heating baths and hypocausts.

The remains of three Roman Villas have been discovered near Wenlock Edge. Wroxeter, the fourth largest city in Britain during the Roman period, was only six miles away; despite this, there is little evidence to suggest that the Romans had a great deal of influence on the woodlands

of the Edge. It is very likely that they continued to be managed very much as they had done in the Iron Age, with coppice products being the main output.

Following the collapse of the Roman Empire around 400AD, Anglo-Saxon tribes took over an England which was already more than half farmland. In some places woodland clearance continued but at a much slower rate than it had done in the previous centuries; there may also have been some woodland recolonisation of marginal agricultural land. The Anglo-Saxons lived mainly in open–field villages but like their predecessors were large users, not only of timber but of coppice for wattle work, structures of many kinds, fencing and fuel. Wood pasture, where animals graze amongst trees, would also have been an important land use but the steepness of the Edge would have made this practice difficult. Overall, the woods would also not have been very valuable for pannage, as there would only be small quantities of oak, it is also unlikely that Beech would have been introduced by this time. It is therefore likely that Wenlock Edge's woodlands would have continued to be largely managed by coppicing, as they had been for the past two thousand years or so, without too much interference by domesticated stock.

What Domesday Book tells us, the Plague and on to the end of the First World War

Domesday Book, produced in 1087 with the results of a survey started only the previous year, indicates that almost all of eleventh-century England was densely settled. Large areas of woodland were very few and many villages had no nearby woodland to exploit. Unfortunately the records for Shropshire are not as good as for most other counties; from these it would appear that only 8% was wooded. This contrasts with Worcestershire, one of the most wooded areas with 40% cover; the overall woodland cover for England has been assessed at around 15%. It is however very likely that Wenlock Edge was one of the few areas in Shropshire to retain significant tree cover.

Further clearance continued over the next 250 years or so, until by 1350 it was reduced to only 10%. This was mainly by the clearance of the larger wooded areas, so it is likely that Shropshire's woodland remained more or less untouched.

Following the Great Plague of 1350 trees began to recolonise abandoned agricultural land, the area of woodland in England returning to around 15% by 1400. From this time, and for most of the next 500 years or so, woodlands would have been managed in a fairly consistent way as coppice with standards. This involved the growing of timber trees, the 'standards' in a matrix of underwood cut (coppiced) on a regular cycle. The presence of a few pollarded limes in the current woodlands on the lower slopes suggests that stock were allowed to graze in these areas; it is unlikely for reasons mentioned earlier that much of the 'upper' woodland would have been used in this way. In most of the areas of coppice, domestic animals would have been kept out so that regrowth would not have been damaged.

The demand for charcoal for smelting in local iron works, and for lime-burning over many centuries, required the woodlands to be managed fairly intensively over long periods. Evidence for the large-scale production of charcoal comes from the presence of many charcoal hearths, saw pits, trackways and other associated features which are found throughout the woods. This work would have required long-term planning to ensure that areas were worked to produce a sustainable output (although that word was probably not used in those days).

The presence across the Edge of a number of Beech of around 150 to 200 years old, with a scattering of 80 to 100 year old Norway Spruce, shows that at least some planting took place during the 19th and early 20th centuries, as neither of these species would be found naturally here. Their location and the fact that they are of open-grown form suggests that they were planted for landscape reasons and not for timber production; it is unlikely that large numbers were used. Other species such as oak may well have also been planted during this period but as they also occur naturally, it is difficult to distinguish between them now.

Pollarded lime

1920 to the mid 1980s – a period of great change

Bluebells quickly re-established in a cleared spruce area where they had not been seen flowering for some 40 years.

Woodland on the Edge had remained relatively 'natural' for around 10,000 years, until the twentieth century (possibly as late as the 1950s and 60s). Some relative small scale introductions such as Beech, Sycamore and Norway Spruce had occurred before this time, probably planted by the Victorians; these would not have greatly affected the overall ecological integrity or landscape of the area. The felling and removal of timber to support the war effort in the First World War, (and probably WWII) would have had some impact. The major changes only happened after the creation of the Forestry Commission in 1920, because of concerns over the reliance of the UK on timber imports. There was a drive to increase the production of conifer timber, both by creating new woodlands on open land and establishing plantations in existing woods such as those on Wenlock Edge. This was either carried out directly by

the Forestry Commission on land it managed itself, or by providing financial incentives for private owners to do it. The costs of creating plantations of introduced trees on Wenlock Edge were very high; without financial incentives provided through the Forestry Commission it would not have been a worthwhile investment for private owners. These practices obviously also had significant effects on the ecological integrity of the woodland, breaking many thousands of years of continuity.

Tree species which were introduced to the Edge during this time included conifers from North West America, such as Douglas Fir, Western Hemlock, Sitka Spruce, Lawson's Cypress, Western Red Cedar, Grand Fir, Lodgepole Pine and even small amounts of Coastal Redwood. Species native to Europe but not the UK, such as Norway Spruce, European Larch and Corsican Pine were also planted.

Beech and Scots Pine are both considered native but their natural distribution does not include Shropshire, so they can also be thought of as being artificially introduced. Although Beech is now found throughout the UK, it is thought that it only reached southern England and just into south-east Wales without help from man. Similarly Scots Pine is now considered truly native only in parts of Scotland although it 'passed' naturally through England on its way north. Japanese Larch was also planted extensively, other species used in relatively small amounts included hybrid poplars, Sweet Chestnut and Southern Beech from South America. The status of Sycamore in the British Isles is open to debate but the majority view is that it is not native; it has probably been a component of the woods on Wenlock Edge for some time. In particular areas it has been encouraged because of its timber value and relative ease of establishment, either through planting or natural seeding.

In less than twenty years from the 1950s the make up of these woodlands therefore shifted from consisting of an almost complete cover of native trees and shrubs, to large areas being dominated by introduced species. These dramatic changes in vegetation cover, the methods used to achieve this and the addition of forestry tracks to improve access, obviously had serious impacts on the existing wildlife, landscape and cultural interests.

In order to maximise timber production, particularly softwood from conifer trees, as much light, water and nutrients as possible must be available. This means controlling all unwanted regrowth from native vegetation (weeds!) which might compete with the timber trees, ensuring that as much light as possible is intercepted to produce wood. If these trees were evergreen and the forester was doing his job properly, then little light was left for anything else and shrubs and ground flora could not thrive. The emphasis on timber production continued until around the mid 1980s, when the unique values of ancient woods and native trees began to be more widely appreciated. The true costs of growing timber on these sites became apparent and owners became less keen to continue with this type of investment.

Sallow Coppice

Late 1980s to 2010 – knowledge, appreciation and change

Ancient woodlands have long been recognised as one of the UK's richest wildlife and cultural resources; conservationists were always aware of the damage that the forestry policy and practices of the mid 20th century was causing. In the late 1980s and early 1990s, greater recognition of the irreplaceable interests of these remnant areas and the damage being caused to them, led to overall changes in approach and attempts to restore what had been lost.

As well as the unique wildlife, cultural and landscape value of places such as Wenlock Edge becoming generally better known, there was a great thirst for increased knowledge about such places so many surveys

Norway Spruce

were undertaken. Biological surveys not only provided information about individual species, communities and habitats existing in the woods, they also enabled areas to be classified into woodland types using nationally recognised methods.

Two main classification schemes exist, Peterken's Stand Types published in 1981 and The National Vegetation Classification (NVC) for Woodlands of 1992. Both schemes attempt to put woodlands into categories depending on the existing/potential natural and semi-natural plant communities, including trees, which are obviously dependent on the location, underlying geology and soil type of the area. The main Woodland type present on the Edge is NVC W8, (Ash, Field Maple and Dog's Mercury). This is a typical woodland community of base-rich soils in the lowlands of southern Britain. There is also some affinity with W9 which is the northern equivalent of W8 with Rowan (Mountain Ash) replacing Field Maple; reflecting the location of Wenlock Edge towards the cooler and wetter north and west of 'lowland' Britain. There are also smaller areas of W10 in flatter places, (Pedunculate Oak, Bracken and Bramble) and small fragments of W7 in wetter areas, (Alder, Ash and Yellow Pimpernel).

Surveys also confirmed that as well as the areas that had remained relatively untouched by forestry practices in the 50s, 60s and 70s, viable remnants of ancient woodland flora survived in the introduced plantations and alongside rides where light levels allowed. It was therefore thought that it might be possible to use these remnants to help recolonise other areas from where they had been lost; the best way would be to slowly remove the introduced trees and allow them to be replaced with native species. Work by National Trust in the late 1980s and early 1990s demonstrated the success of this approach; Bluebells quickly re-established in a cleared spruce area where they had not been seen flowering for some 40 years. Naturally regenerating Ash seedlings and other seed-bearing species nearby were also quick to colonise these open areas, showing that it would be relatively easy to recreate natural woodland without the need for planting.

Being able to work slowly and phase the work over a period of years has a number of advantages over trying to 'restore' native woodland quickly. The flora of ancient woodlands has taken hundreds and even thousands of years to develop, in association with tree cover; many of the most important and valuable species cannot disperse easily. They are therefore slow to take opportunities to move into new suitable areas; too much light may allow more aggressive and less valuable 'weed' species in that change the balance of the plant communities. Once this has happened it is very difficult if not impossible to restore the ancient woodland flora.

Another benefit of this approach is that it enables the produce of the operations; timber, fencing material, firewood etc to be sold when markets allow. The income can be used to support the restoration work, respects the original investment in time and money that created these stands and provides products with excellent carbon credentials.

The restoration work is also supported by grant aid from the Forestry Commission, ironic, as they encouraged the conversion to conifer plantations in the first place, less than half a century ago. This demonstrates how government and society changes the way they value woodlands; 50 years is a relatively short period in the life of a tree and particularly of a woodland. If maximum

Hazeldine Coppice

long-term benefits are to be achieved then long-term continuity of purpose is required!

The benefits of leaving some areas untouched and allowing natural processes to work has also been recognised. This type of 'management' is commonly referred to as non-intervention.

10,000 years of trees on Wenlock Edge but what is there now?

Today's tree cover on Wenlock Edge is the result of many contributing factors, both natural and interventions by man over a long period. Natural aspects such as the soil and underlying geology continue to influence plant diversity and tree growth but there is very little, if any, of the existing woodland structure that has not been significantly affected by man's activities. Whilst some natural and man-made features of past tree cover have been lost, there is still plenty of evidence for how the woodlands reached the condition they are in today. The woods along the Edge are now owned and managed by organisations including National Trust, the Forestry Commission and Shropshire Wildlife Trust and also by private individuals. These owners have different aims for their woodlands, this will continue to influence their development. What we see now provides links with the various states the tree cover has gone through over the millennia.

Speller Coppice

The Conifers

At present, it is very obvious that significant parts of the woodland area are dominated by conifer plantations, most of which are less than 60 years old. Some have grown well and have produced good timber, others have proved to be a poor investment. Although not ideally suited to the local soil conditions, Douglas Fir, Japanese and European Larch have contributed acceptable timber yields and financial returns. They also provide attractive areas to walk through where they have been well managed, with the individual trees given plenty of space to grow and light allowed to reach the ground beneath to benefit native plants. Less successful have been Sitka Spruce and Western Hemlock, as they do not like alkaline soils. Their premature removal has generally cost money rather than producing an income. Other conifers which have partially succeeded include Scots Pine, Norway Spruce, Grand Fir, Western Red Cedar and Lawson's Cypress.

Current policy will lead to a gradual removal of conifers and replacement with native woodland; over the Edge there will be areas at different stages in this process for many years. It is not the intention to remove all the conifers, the retention of some of the better individual trees and groves will be a reminder for a long time of this phase of tree cover.

Introduced Broadleaves

Beech is the most dominant of the introduced broadleaved trees, although considered native further south, it may not have arrived naturally in Shropshire but undoubtedly would have done eventually. Most of the oldest Beech on the Edge are around 150 to 200 years old, mainly concentrated along the top of the slope, having developed in fairly open conditions. In some places these Beeches can now be found within the wood, still with the

Hazel coppice stool

lower branches and form of trees that started their lives with more space, indicating that the woodland that now surrounds them is of more recent origin.

There are also significant Beech plantations established in the mid 20th century to produce timber. Some of these have been well-managed and, because they have been grown close together, have the potential to produce fine, clean stemmed timber trees. Because of the dense shade that they cast, the ground flora is unlikely to be as rich as in Ash-dominated areas; over many years it will develop a unique character adding to the overall diversity. It is also predicted that climate change will lead to the decline of Beech trees in the south east of England and so having fine stands in Shropshire, where it is thought that conditions will be more suitable, will enable people to continue to enjoy them.

Although the status and origins of Sycamore are still debated, it tends to be more invasive than Beech. Given opportunities it can dominate, generally to the detriment of the wildlife of ancient woodlands. There are areas on the Edge where it has become dominant, indeed some where it has been encouraged, as it does produce fine and valuable timber; at the moment it is generally being kept in check by the existing tree cover. The removal of conifer plantations to restore native tree cover will give opportunities for Sycamore to establish but good practice can reduce this threat.

There is not much Sweet (Spanish) Chestnut in the woods but small areas can be found scattered over the Edge. In the right places they grow well, producing valuable timber from maiden trees and excellent naturally-durable fencing products from coppicing. They also make fantastic old trees when their bark starts to become deeply fissured and often twisted. The decaying heartwood is also valuable for fungi and insects. As in many woodlands, there are also a small number of Horse Chestnuts that have been planted over the years for amenity reasons; it is unlikely that they will ever contribute significantly to the area, apart from the odd local 'special' tree.

Poplars are normally found growing on flat areas with a high water table, near to water bodies such as streams and lakes, surprisingly there are a few noticeable areas on the lower slopes of the Edge. These commercial plantings tend to be on less freely draining, deeper soils and were probably planted when poplar timber was in demand during the 1970s and 80s. They have grown reasonably well, creating their own unique landscape; it is unlikely that they will make the financial returns predicted when they were planted. These hybrid poplars are bred to produce timber quickly and do not live long, normally blowing over or breaking apart if they are not felled by the time they are 40 to 50 years old. They can regrow from stumps or from natural sets, so tend to perpetuate themselves once established unless steps are taken to prevent this. The only native poplar species present in the woodlands on the Edge is Aspen. Not many are found, despite its habit of forming small groves through suckering.

Two other introduced trees that can be found in small numbers are Hornbeam (native to southern England) and Southern Beech (native to South America). Hornbeam (able to live in the shade) can live for centuries, developing in to wonderful ancient trees. Southern Beech would have been planted as a timber tree, now it just provides evidence of a failed experiment and is not expected to remain standing or live to any great age.

Hazel coppice

The cutting of Hazel on Wenlock Edge has probably been going on for over 5,000 years and continues today. The best Hazel coppice is cut every 7 to 8 years, needing plenty of light to enable it to grow straight and quickly to produce the most valuable poles. Where there is too high a density of trees above and around the coppice, growth is slow and crooked and the vigour of the stool reduces. Regular cutting of Hazel and the more light reaching the ground benefits the many plants and associated dependent fauna which could otherwise suffer.

If Hazel is not cut then over a number of years the older growth starts to bend outwards and younger shoots grow up straight from the middle. Woodmen often refer to coppice in this state as being 'neglected'. Although the financial value of the products is diminished, very old stools have their own wildlife interests and are often visually wonderful. Over the Edge it is possible to see active and neglected coppice areas; the overall wildlife and landscape interests are enhanced by having both.

The Current Dominant Tree

The tree which would naturally dominate most of the Edge today is the Ash. It is very much at home with the soil conditions and seeds prolifically, meaning that it is very able to colonise open areas. There are not many old Ash trees, no doubt because they were removed and sold when the plantations of the 1950s and 60s were created. Whilst Ash timber is very versatile and has been used for many purposes, it was discriminated against during the mid 20th century when the drive to produce conifer timber was at its height. On Wenlock Edge there would have been a great effort to control Ash growth when trying to establish the conifer plantations. As we now know, this was mostly a waste of time and money; in the struggle between man and nature there would only be

one sensible long term winner. Ash is a light–demander, not regenerating well in dense woodland. It produces good timber and excellent firewood, coppices well and is easy to grow; the ideal 'commercial' tree for the Edge. Others might rate it more highly for its value to wildlife, particularly as it does not cast a dense shade and allows lower plants to flourish beneath it. Whatever way you look at it, growing Ash on Wenlock Edge makes sense.

The only problem with Ash is that its prolific regeneration from seed often leads to young trees growing very closely together. They grow tall and spindly, are prone to canker and do not have the capability of becoming a fine tree, or of long life. This can be overcome by thinning the trees when they are young enough to respond to extra room to develop. The amount of space the tree has over the years will determine whether and how quickly it will produce small sized roundwood, high quality large timber or even develop into an open grown veteran living for perhaps 300 years.

Past Domination

Ash may be the most dominant native tree now but three species: Wych Elm, Small Leaved Lime and Large Leaved Lime, which in past times would have covered large areas of the Edge, can still be found today. Unlike Ash, these three species can all tolerate shade and are well adapted to living in dense woodland. Once established they would have dominated woodlands for long periods of time unless disturbed.

There are few if any large Wych Elm trees that have survived Dutch Elm

Ash plantation and thinnings for fire wood

Aspen

small timbers, now for cultural and wildlife interests. From the size of their bollings (trunks) they are probably at least 300 years old. The multi-stemmed trees were probably felled during clearing work and have regrown from the cut stumps, whether this was wanted or not and some may have been deliberately poisoned to prevent this, allowing more 'valuable' trees to take their place. We now appreciate the contribution they make to the woodlands and remind us of past tree cover.

A few more native trees to look for

Although oak trees do not occupy large areas, where they do grow they are of significant timber and wildlife value. Both Pedunculate Oak and Sessile Oak are present; any natural variation in their distribution is likely to have been obscured by planting. There are very few large or ancient oaks along the Edge, they tend to be on the lower slopes as spreading trees, indicating that they have grown outside the woodlands in the past. Some of the best oak and hazel wood is found in Long Coppice, a relatively flat area where the soils are much deeper and more fertile. There is also a nice area to the north of Harley Hill on a very steep slope.

Disease; abundant regrowth from stumps and seedlings in the lower canopy are reminders of when it contributed much more tree cover. Because of the recurring nature of the disease it is unlikely that large Elm trees will feature again for a long time.

Individual surviving specimens of Small and Large-leaved Limes (and possibly natural hybrids of the two), bear testament to when they would have been more widespread and to their resilience to man's activities. Very few maiden trees are known, limes are found mainly in two forms, pollarded and multi-stemmed. The former are the result of planned activities designed to perpetuate and conserve them, originally as fodder for animals and

The Wild Cherry or Gean likes light and so is generally found on the edge of woodlands, its bright white blossom being a common sight in spring. Gean has the ability to sucker from roots, so where it has sufficient light and space it often forms small groves, sometimes with similar aged stems and sometimes trees of various ages, these can be really striking features. Although close-grown cherry trees generally do not have long lives, their wood is much sought-after for high quality furniture.

Yew trees can survive in quite dark situations and live for many centuries if not millennia. Their main concentrations tend to be alongside tracks but there are

Timber products
from Wenlock Edge
woodlands, made at
Acton Scott Museum

The Living Edge – A wanderer's guide to Wenlock Edge · National Trust

also scattered individuals, the oldest are probably well over 500 years old.

Other native trees which have arrived in the woods without man's assistance include Holly, Birch, Field Maple, Hawthorn, various willow species, Rowan and Crab Apple; these tend to exist as individuals or in small groups and do not dominate significant areas. As previously mentioned, Aspen is also present in small numbers, both as individual trees and as suckering groups.

The most ancient of all

When looking for past evidence of woodland on Wenlock Edge, the trees that are currently growing tell us very little, we cannot see the wood for the trees. The fact that individual areas are called woods or coppices tells us that these have been worked for centuries. If we want confirmation of tree cover here before they were even named we must look below the trees at the smaller woody plants and the ground. Here we find the species only found in true Ancient Woodlands, plants that need long continuity of native tree cover to thrive, like the Wild Service, Spurge Laurel, Bluebells, Woodruff, Herb Paris, Wood Anemone, Pendulous Sedge and other such Ancient Woodland Indicator plants. These have survived the thousands of years of tree management and other activities of man, confirming that there has been significant continuous tree cover on Wenlock Edge for a very, very long time. Individual trees, stands and even species come and go but the woodland, and the flora and fauna that it supports, remains and will continue to dominate the Edge for the foreseeable future.

Woodlands: The Future

The story so far

Although there has been tree cover on the Edge for thousands of years, today's woods are unique, different to anything that has gone before and continuing to change. During the past 10,000 years both natural and human activities have played a part in determining the type of tree cover. But what will be the main causes of future change and what type of tree cover is likely to exist at the end of the 21st century?

Doing nothing for ninety years

What would happen if the woods were abandoned and left to change without human interference? Apart from the paths, rides and railway line becoming overgrown, very little change would be seen for perhaps twenty years. Trees would continue to grow with natural seedlings filling the gaps, resulting in the wood gradually becoming denser and darker. This would begin to impact on the wildlife dependant on open areas and light, particularly flowering species and insects. Hazel and other woody shrub species would also decline. Veteran trees such as lime pollards and open-grown Beech trees would begin to suffer from competition from faster-growing younger trees. Conifers would gradually die standing or blow over; the gaps would be filled with natural regeneration of other trees or shrubs. Ash would continue to dominate, forming very dense stands with tall unstable trees vulnerable to windblow and ash canker, being so close together. Oaks need lots of light

and space to regenerate and their dominance in areas would gradually decline, whereas Beech is more shade-tolerant. Other native species that could benefit from the darker conditions are Holly, Yew, Lime and Wych Elm. Most introduced conifer species prefer open situations, so their dominance would reduce, native species taking their place. Western Hemlock is the exception, surviving and regenerating in quite shady conditions. The amount of standing and fallen deadwood would increase, benefiting the fungi and insects that live on or in it. Mammals such as deer and Grey Squirrels would increase and their damaging effects on tree regeneration and development escalate.

At the end of the 21st century there would still be a wood on the Edge, albeit much denser with few surviving large open-grown trees. Shrub species and ground flora would be reduced and their dependant fauna greatly impoverished. It would still support wildlife specially adapted to dense woodland and undisturbed areas. Access would be difficult, the evidence of past human activities obscured and slowly disappearing. The amount of carbon being released by decaying wood would be approaching that being taken up by growing trees. The Edge would eventually become carbon neutral and not a net sequester as it had been at the beginning of the 21st century.

Producing wood

Over the past 5,000 years or so, man has manipulated the growing trees on the Edge to provide the resources needed to survive and improve his way of life. The

woodlands are now valued for their contribution to the landscape, for informal recreation and as an important site for wildlife. It would be surprising if these did not remain long-term aims. Trees aid soil and water conservation and lock up carbon, these benefits vary; native species being better for soil and water conservation, faster-growing introduced trees sequestering carbon more quickly. It is only recently that the trees on the Edge have been appreciated for their landscape, access and wildlife qualities; for thousands of years it was woodland products that were most valued. A desire to reduce our environmental footprint and increase the use of products with better carbon credentials, including woodfuel, will result in a greater demand for these products, particularly those of local origin. Security of supply will also be important, as importing resources is likely to become more expensive and difficult. Is there a way to remove increased amounts of woody material for overall environmental benefits, whilst maintaining the long term values of Wenlock

Edge? Knowledge of the requirements of the indigenous wildlife and wood production is also needed.

In order for trees to live, they need to grow and this produces wood. Different species grow at different rates depending on the local conditions, soil type, rainfall, etc. Taking into account the area of woodland on the Edge and the native and other species growing there, the amount of wood being produced every year is in excess of 3,000 cubic metres. It would therefore be possible to sustainably remove around 2,500 cubic metres of wood annually and still leave a good proportion for wildlife, both in the form of old trees and standing and fallen deadwood. Replanting felled areas in established woodlands can be difficult and expensive, but on the Edge, regeneration will come from natural seeding and coppice regrowth at minimum cost. It would therefore be easy to produce a sustainable harvest in the long term, based predominantly on Ash and Hazel with Beech, oak and other species contributing. Ash produces very versatile timber and excellent fuelwood and can be managed to provide different products. Being a native species and not casting a dense shade, Ash is also excellent for wildlife and is a lovely tree to walk amongst.

Potential threats and consequences

Much has been written about how our climate might change over the 21st century and how this could affect tree cover. There is much uncertainty about climate change predictions; the mean annual temperature may increase by 3 to 6°C, perhaps more in the winter than the summer, with a substantial decrease in the number of frosty days. Summer rainfall may fall by up to 50%, winter rainfall increasing by 10 to 40%; summer droughts and winter flooding becoming more common. There is likely to be an increase in the occurrence of storms.

Shropshire, being in northwest of England may experience less extreme climate change. The north-west facing aspect of Wenlock Edge, terrain, soil type and underlying geology mean that its trees may be little affected by drought or waterlogging. Tree growth in Shropshire may even increase as the temperature rises, if the growing season lengthens and sufficient summer rainfall still falls. Evolution will also play its part, ensuring that young trees will have genetic variations, making them more or less suited to the changing conditions. The tree cover will adapt over time; species like Ash which produce large numbers of cross-fertilised seedlings with

genetic variation may benefit, whereas other species that propagate through vegetative means such as coppiced Hazel may struggle. Whilst the possible impact of climate change itself is unlikely to have a negative effect on trees on the Edge, there will inevitably be some changes in the relative abundance of particular species.

As well as possible changes to tree health and growth, climate change is likely to benefit the pests and diseases which affect them, with new ones appearing. Stressed trees are more vulnerable to attack; this should not be too great a problem for native trees on the Edge, particularly those that reproduce prolifically through seeding. Physical damage, particularly to young trees, may worsen as deer and Grey Squirrels increase due to the milder winters. Young Ash seedlings are vulnerable to deer browsing; Beech, Sycamore and some other tree species can be damaged or killed by the bark stripping of Grey Squirrels. Deer can also impact negatively on coppice regrowth, shrubs and important ground flora species such as Bluebells. Control of these animals may be necessary.

What is likely to happen

The woods provide a varied mix of material products such as timber and fuel wood, with other benefits including wildlife and informal access. Throughout the UK there will be an increasing demand for local wood products and services; there are three main attributes which make the woodlands on Wenlock Edge suitable to produce a sustainable supply of these. The first is the overall size of the area, meaning that large parts can be worked without causing major disruption to wildlife or access. Big landscapes can cope with extensive working, this brings economies of scale allowing the efficient removal of products, making reasonable returns on operations.

The second is good machinery access routes that help to keep costs down. The third is simply good tree growth on the Edge which will allow continual removal of products and their replacement.

As they have done for thousands of years, the woodlands on Wenlock Edge will continue to supply renewable goods and services during the 21st century and beyond. The structure and species makeup will inevitably change during the rest of this century; it is unlikely that there will be significant areas of conifer trees left by 2100, although there may be some very interesting old specimens of Larch, Scots Pine and Douglas Fir scattered through the woods. Broadleaved trees and shrubs will dominate and as well as the areas that are being commercially worked, management will ensure that large old specimens of Lime, Oak, Beech, Ash and other species survive. Native evergreen species such as Yew and Holly will be more extensive, providing protection and food for mammals and birds during the winter. Large-scale coppicing of Ash and Hazel will continue to produce the conditions necessary for wildlife to thrive. Timber will also be taken on a regular basis but significant areas will have been left alone, favouring the wildlife which likes darker, undisturbed woodland conditions and quantities of deadwood.

From a distance, the slow changes in the structure of the woodlands will hardly have been noticed, the trees on the Edge will still be the most prominent feature in the local landscape. Changes in land use may allow woodlands to expand down the hill to reclaim some of the agricultural land. This spread would improve water courses, the soil and wildlife as well as increasing overall wood production.

Walking within the woods would remain an important recreational activity; the changes which improve wildlife values would enhance this enjoyment. The woodlands would be more attractive in the spring if more light encourages more ground flora. Bluebells would flourished and be more abundant. Maintenance of paths and rides would result in more people using the woods as a wonderful place to improve their physical and mental wellbeing.

Although the woods that clothe the Edge at the end of the 21st Century would be different, humans from 4,000 years ago and from more recent times would recognise familiar features and activities. Many tree species and other plants would be the same. This is testimony to the enduring nature of woods such as those on Wenlock Edge and their continuing value to the human race.

The Natural Year

By Pete Carty

Many of the habitats found around Wenlock Edge, such as Ancient Broadleaved woodland, flower-rich hay meadow and open quarry grassland are increasingly rare. They are vital to the diverse range of plants and animals which live here. However some species have been lost and others struggle to survive. Careful management of this landscape is needed to ensure that they continue to exist.

Mid – late march

As catkins of Pussy Willow and Hazel announce the end of winter, Dog's Mercury is one of the first woodland flowers to appear. The striking white flowers of Blackthorn also appear at this time along the wood edge and the hedgerows.

The first Chiffchaffs arrive from Africa and start to sing in tall trees; our resident thrushes, Robins and Chaffinches are singing everywhere. They are joined by Treecreepers, Greenfinches and by the thin song of Goldcrests where there are evergreen trees. In the hedgerows listen for the characteristic song of the Yellowhammer, asking for "a little bit of bread and no cheese". Great Spotted Woodpeckers don't sing, instead they find a branch that will vibrate when hammered with their powerful bills, this is known as drumming.

In the sky, Ravens are croaking and displaying, Buzzards and Peregrines are there too; Red Kites are heading this way and will be seen more regularly.

Left: **Yellowhammer**
Above: **Cowslip**
Below: **Blackthorn blossom**

April

The lovely Wood Anemones and Wood Sorrel appear; both indicators of ancient woodland. Along the sunlit banks and glades, Primroses are like beacons of colour. Also look out for Opposite-leafed Golden Saxifrage, Violets and Lesser Celandine, the latter was used as a cure for haemorrhoids. The leaves of Lords and Ladies appear but the flowers are much later. Toads, frogs and newts come to the pools to breed, often in large numbers. Towards the end of the month there are displays of Cowslips in the meadows and old quarries e.g. in the Stokes Barn area and Ippikins Meadow opposite the Wenlock Edge Inn.

The wood turns from bare to bright fresh green foliage. Summer birds arrive from Africa and the woodland chorus is added to with Blackcaps, Garden Warblers and Willow Warblers. In the quarries, Redstart and Wheatear are occasional breeders.

May

This is the month for great shows of woodland flowers; Yellow Archangel and Greater Stitchwort appear in the woods along with the first Bluebells and swathes of Wild Garlic leaves. The leaves of the garlic make excellent soup and Stitchwort is reputed to be a cure for the stitch in your side. You have to wait until late May for the spectacle of Wild Garlic flowers (Ippikins Rock is a good place to see them). Bluebells turn some sections of the woods completely blue e.g. at Stanway Coppice or Coats Wood. Wall Brown butterflies can also be found around rocky places in late May; solitary bees and wasps are busy going in and out of nest holes in the crumbling quarry banks.

Top: **Wood Anemone**
Left: **Wood Sorrel**
Right: **Solitary bee**

June

June is a spectacle of flowers in the unshaded grasslands, quarries and hedgebanks. In open ground along the bare quarry edge Bird's-foot Trefoil is busy turning nitrogen into fertiliser, this in turn allows other plant species to invade. Wild Strawberries are out and make a tasty wild snack. There is a profusion of orchids, with Early Purple and Twayblade in the woods and later, Common Spotted, Bee, Butterfly and towards the month end, Pyramidal orchids. The latter often in profusion with the spectacular Vipers Bugloss. There is the delicate lemon yellow of Lemon Mouse Ear, the only lemon yellow dandelion type flower.

In the meadows and old quarries the parasitic Yellow Rattle is suppressing the tall grasses, allowing smaller herbs to thrive amongst finer grasses e.g. Quaking Grass.

Late June – early July

There is Greater Knapweed, Red Campion, Yellow-wort, Eyebright, Fairy Flax, Carline Thistle, Wild Thyme and great shows of Dog Daisy in the quarries. You can smell the flowers of the Lime trees and notice the bees attracted to them. In Ippikins Meadow Dyers Green Weed and Ladies Bedstraw are in bloom with Common Centaury, Cut Leaved Mallow and Common Gromwell.

In the dark corners of the wood other orchids; Broad Leaved, Dark Red and Narrow Lipped Helleborines come into flower. These can grow in deep shade due to their relationship with a fungal partner in their roots which provide food.

In late June a woodland glade butterfly, the Ringlet, is on the wing; caterpillars are common on the leaves of trees, particularly those of Geometrid moths, often called inch worms.

Late July and August

Wenlock Edge's flower show continues well into August depending on the weather. Whilst there are usually plenty of flowers out, there are the first signs of summer coming to end; watch out for the Autumn Gentian along the top of Lea Quarry and early fungi emerging a few days after rain. Silver Washed Fritillaries nectar on thistles along the hedgerows.

Opposite page
Left: **Bee Orchid**
Top left: **Greater Butterfly Orchid**
Top middle: **Vipers Bugloss**
Top right: **Pyramidal Orchid**
Bottom left: **Mouse-ear Hawkweed**
Bottom right: **Eyebright**

Top: **Greater Knapweed**
Above: **Ringlet Butterfly**
Right: **Silver-washed Fritillary Butterfly**

September

This is a time for wild fruits, hazelnuts, blackberries and also fungi (if you are interested in fungi then join one of the fungal forays organised locally). Birds are migrating with summer visitors departing and winter birds arriving; it is an exciting time when unusual species may turn up.

October and November

Leaves turn to autumn colours, Ash, the dominant tree along the edge, rarely shows good colour but others do e.g. Oak, Larch, Sycamore and Beech. This is often a good time to look at mosses and lichens. Look for Hazel nuts nibbled by mice, voles and squirrels, the teeth marks tell which species has eaten the nut. The winter Thrushes, Redwings and Fieldfares arrive and you might see a Brambling.

December to February

Watch out for the hoar frost and ice shaped by biting winds and the lovely clear light allowing views across Shropshire. It's a good time to test your tree identification i.e. by their winter shape and twigs.

If it snows, get up early and follow the tracks of the woodland inhabitants and see where they travelled in the night. Badger, Fox, deer and birds all leave their marks. Small birds like tits and Goldcrests roam the woods in mixed flocks.

Redwing

Acknowledgments

With a book such as this which has been a collaborative effort there are many people to thank, these include:

The authors:
Paul Evans, Dr Peter Toghill, Dr Ian Dormor, Glyn Williams, Dr Sara Whild, Dr Caroline Uff, Leo Smith, John Hughes and Ray Hawes.

We have drawn on original unpublished work on Wenlock Edge woodlands by Will Prestwood and Terry Merchant and archaeology by Jeremy Milln. Ken Milner has been generous with his extensive local knowledge of flora and history. Paul Francis and Amy Douglas produced original work which for reasons of space has not been included in the final publication. Amy has just published a collection of folk stories.

Initial text editing Barbara Vickery.

Pete and Kate Johnson collated photographs and coordinated photography and did much to shape the book.

Book design and artwork by **MA Creative**, Shrewsbury.
www.macreative.co.uk

Map of dormouse distribution produced by Alex Lockton with data provided by Shropshire Mammal Society and Shropshire Wildlife Trust.

For general support and help my National Trust colleagues.

And last but not least special thanks to Alistair Heath, NT Area Ranger who has planned, managed, sold timber and sweated at Wenlock Edge for 15 years and Chris Dunkerley his assistant who has similarly worked for seven years. You can check out week to week work at Chris's blog.
www.wenlockedgenationaltrust.blogspot.com

Both Chris and Al have contributed knowledge and experience into the pages of this book but were too busy in the woods to write it themselves.

Peter Carty
Countryside, Park and Garden Manager
National Trust, South Shropshire

Alistair Heath and
Chris Dunkerley
NT Rangers Wenlock Edge

The Authors

Paul Evans
The Living Edge, and Landscape & Seasons: Winter, Spring, Summer and Autumn
Paul Evans is a nature writer, radio broadcaster and lecturer based in Much Wenlock.

Dr Peter Toghill
Geology
Peter Toghill has lived in Church Stretton since 1971. For 30 years he was a Lecturer in Earth Sciences at the University of Birmingham. He initiated the founding of the Shropshire Geological Society in 1979 and is now its Vice-President. He has published two successful books, *Geology of Britain* and *Geology of Shropshire*, in 2001 he received an international award from the Geological Society of London for promoting the public understanding of Geology. For the last 10 years he and his colleagues in the Shropshire Geological Society have been running successful geological walks for National Trust in Shropshire.

Dr Ian Dormor
Archaeology & Landscape History
Ian Dormor is a landscape historian. Prior to his retirement he was Landscape Conservation Officer for the Shropshire Hills AONB Partnership. Ian's doctorate from Leeds University was awarded for his research on the landscape history of the Yorkshire Dales woodlands.

Glyn Williams
Limestone Industry
Retired Primary School Headteacher, Glyn was born in Much Wenlock and, apart from college days and two stints in the armed forces, has lived in the town all of his life. Much has been written about the historic town of Much Wenlock, but nothing was recorded about the town's limestone industry. Over the last twenty years or so, Glyn has tried to rectify this resulting in the publication in 1997 of *The Wenlock Limestone Industry*.

Pete Carty
Grassland and Natural Year
Peter Carty has had a lifelong interest in wildlife and the environment. In the past Peter has managed nature reserves in Orkney, Seychelles, Barrow in Furness and Merseyside. He now works for National Trust in Shropshire.

Dr Sarah Whild
Plants & Vegetation
Sarah Whild is Lecturer in Plant Ecology for the University of Birmingham and has lived and botanized in Shropshire for 30 years. Sarah has been Chair of the Shropshire Botanical Society and is the BSBI's (Botanical Society of the British Isles) recorder for the county. She has produced publications on Rare Plants of Shropshire, and Floras of Attingham Park, Haughmond Hill, Stiperstones and Shrewsbury and she is working on a new edition of the *Flora of Shropshire*.

The Authors

Dr Caroline Uff
Wildlife

Following a career in cancer research, Caroline chose to pursue her love of wildlife and now works as the property ecologist for National Trust, South Shropshire.

Leo Smith
Birds

Leo Smith has been surveying, mapping and writing about the birds of the Shropshire hills, promoting their conservation for over 25 years. This has been his major occupation since he retired from a career in Local Government in 2002, and moved to Bishop's Castle.

John Hughes
Fungi

John Hughes has been fascinated by fungi for 30 years. He regularly leads autumn walks around Shropshire's woodlands. He works for Shropshire Wildlife Trust and is regularly to be heard on local radio pontificating on all aspects of wildlife.
www.shropshirewildlifetrust.org.uk

Ray Hawes
Woodlands

Ray Hawes was bought up amongst the Chiltern beechwoods in Buckinghamshire and developed a love of trees and wood at an early age. He has been involved in woodland management since 1976 and has been a Forestry Adviser/Head of Forestry with National Trust since 1989.

Barbara Vickery
Editor

Barbara first fell in love with the Shropshire Hills when she was 30, but had to wait a couple of decades before she could finally fulfill a dream and re-locate to Church Stretton. Her professional background in publications, and in particular, her love for the Long Mynd, made her an obvious choice to help edit the first National Trust book 'Wild Mynd', so helping with the follow-up on Wenlock Edge was a natural progression. She is very involved in many local organisations which benefit the community and is well known as a lover of the hills, where she walks as much as possible.

Pete and Kate Johnson

After a working life in radio presentation and production, Pete and Kate are now pursuing their enthusiasm for natural history and photography.

Photographers

Geoff Taylor
www.geofftaylorphotography.com
Living at the foot of Wenlock Edge, Geoff pursues an enduring passion for the landscape and landscape photography. Further images are shown on his website, many available as fine art prints. He is also employed as a photography tutor with the Open College of the Arts.
PAGES Front Cover, 1, 4, 6, 10, 11, 15, 16, 18, 19, 20, 22, 23, 40, 44, 54, 57, 97, 99, 104, 106, 108, 109, 110, 148, 151, 152, 172, 176, 181, 183, 184, 205, 206, 212, Back Cover

Pete Johnson
PAGES 13, 14, 27, 28, 29, 30, 31, 32, 35, 39, 42, 43, 49, 53, 55, 56, 58, 60, 63, 66, 70, 71, 77, 79, 81, 85, 86, 88, 90, 98, 100, 101, 111, 114, 120, 123, 152,155, 158, 162, 165, 174, 175, 177, 178, 179, 180, 182, 185, 187, 188, 189, 190, 191, 192, 193, 194, 195, 196, 198, 201, 210. 34 & 38 Courtesy of **Ludlow Museum**

Pete Carty
PAGES 73, 81, 87, 88, 91, 92, 93, 95, 98, 100, 102, 158, 164, 192, 194, 200, 202, 203

Kate Johnson
PAGES 12, 21, 36, 55, 78, 88, 107, 114, 124, 150, 153, 154, 158, 159, 160, 162, 164, 165, 168, 175, 186, 189, 197, 204

Mike Ashton
www.macreative.co.uk
Graphic Designer, photographer and wildlife enthusiast, Mike set up **MA Creative** in 1996. He specialises in design work for community and environmental projects.
PAGES 94, 95,102, 119, 120, 122, 123, 124, 139, 141, 155, 156, 160, 161, 168, 169, 170, 171, 201, 209, 210

Mark Sisson
www.marksissonphoto.co.uk
Professional Wildlife Photographer, Shropshire based and with a programme of nature photography workshops and holidays through **Natures Images**
PAGES 110, 114, 116, 203

Glenn Bishton and John Lightfoot
http://shropshirebarnowl group.org.uk
Local ornithologists, photographers and co-founders of The **Shropshire Barn Owl Group**. The group conducts surveys and promotes conservation of barn owls and their habitats throughout the county.
PAGES 122, 123, 124, 125, 200

Gareth Thomas FRPS
www.catswhiskersstudio.com
PAGES 129, 133, 134, 135, 143, 144, 204

Tony Hamblin FRPS
PAGES 126, 133, 134, 136

Peter Beasley ARPS
PAGE 138

Roy Blewitt FRPS
PAGE 137

Peter Toghill
PAGES 26, 33

Ian Dormor
PAGES 53

Glyn Williams
PAGES 66, 72

John Hughes
PAGES 158, 160, 162, 163, 166, 167, 168, 210

John Barnard
PAGES 8, 26

Robin Jukes Hughes
www.shropshirehills photography.com
PAGES 24, 102, 202

English Heritage
www.englishheritageimages. com PAGE 47

Dudley Museum
PAGES 34, 35

Dave Herbert
PAGES 64, 65, 67, 68

John Kane
PAGE 72

National Trust
PAGES 74, 75, 208

Alistair Heath
PAGE 80

Nick Robinson
PAGES 86, 88, 89, 93, 101, 102, 200, 202

Nick Turland
www.flickr.com/nturland
PAGE 90

Chris Stratton
PAGES 117, 167

Danny Beath
www.flickr.com/ flickering_velvet
PAGES 121, 201, 203

Nigel Jones
www.flickr.com/insectman
PAGES 122, 125

David Williams
PAGE 123

Tony Jacques
PAGE 123

Ernie Janes
PAGE 130

Chris Dunkerley
PAGE 192